MW01037068

Praise for Author and Work:

"You express yourself well on these pages. I believe that your readers will be delighted to read what you have shared. I've not read poetry set up like this before and found it refreshing. I expect your readers will be looking for more from you in the days ahead."
-Terry Jacobs, Manuscript Review Specialist, Outskirts Press, Inc.

"Extremely Talented Wordsmith. Scholarly with his Word-Play."
- Tony Watson, Rhema Records

"Wow, Congratulations Randall. We met about 10 years or so ago in a business capacity. I never imagined you were a talented writer. Your collection of Poetry and Children's writings are going to take the world by storm. Looking forward to your success!"
-Brent Boyd, BANA STUDIOS

"There are times when an artist is able to speak to the reader on levels unknown. Randall is one of those authors. His works are an eclectic collection of works that will speak to your soul. As a professional who has produced many events in the genre of poetry, I've rarely come across such talent. Engaging in his works is something any reader should not miss."
- Maria Cavallaro, Ovations ENT Grp, Poetry Slam Talent Evaluator

A client requested I read this book. It is beautifully written with love, passion, memories, and emotions from the heart. Capturing what once was and what could be. A great read that couples can share together for relationship building. But a must read for all that will allow your mind to roam free.
- Darlene Eisert, DDE, Relationship Coach

A True Poetic Love Story

You Can BE, Who You Can SEE

Stirring Poetry

Hip Hop Memories

<u>For children</u>

Great Britton

Toothbrush Tales

Edited by Evelyn L. Suesberry

"Simply, the most talented Author for whom I have edited."

POETRY THAT MOVES YOU

Paperback   ISBN 978-1-955798-00-6

eBook   ISBN 978-1-955798-01-3

Hip Hop Memories is a

Registered Trademark of Randall Daniels

U.S. Serial Number: 90189418

Author Website

www.RandallDanielsBooks.com

Printed in the United States of America

POETRY THAT MOVES YOU

Randall Daniels

Connect with me:

www.RandallDanielsBooks.com

& Follow Me:

Dedication

I dedicate this book to my Mom, Bobbie Bobo Daniels, who died at the young age of 32. Due to an unforeseen condition, she left four children & I was the 7-year-old little boy. I've yearned for my Mother my entire life. Her love her hugs her kisses & her courage. But her love was a seed she brilliantly planted firmly inside us.

Her seed never left me and her love never died.

The seed she deposited gave comfort when I cried.

With every thought or tear it still seems like she knows,

After millions of tears over my years, her love seed still grows.

To my Mom's Mom, Grandma Marguerite Bobo, thank you for the love and dedication becoming a surrogate Mother. When I was a 25-year-old lad homeless without a Mom or Dad. She didn't hesitate to sneak me in her Senior Center and gave me a place to lay my head. She always believed my brighter days ahead would come… She was right.

I helped bury Grandma, from my 6-figure income.

My **Love** For Your **Love & Help** Grandma.

This book came true and is dedicated to the two of you!!

CONTENTS

LOVE AND ROMANCE

Who's That Girl

I'm sending this letter with no name or address, just simply directed to that girl

That Girl,

I laid awake one Thursday night because my heart wasn't feeling right. A little puzzle was a mystery to me, I didn't know if it could really be. A feeling I had sometime before, a feeling that's definitely not in store, no time soon and that's a fact! My heart and mind will put an end to that. The two together they're so very tight, most conversation they don't even bite. Lost a loved one at seven or so, it made them age, made them really grow. Saw many tears but now they're strong, a love barrier followed along. My heart sealed with nails and screw, but somehow, someway, you broke through!

Signed, Yours Truly.

Who's that girl that made me open my heart, and write this letter that's a form of art.

She had charisma and so much style,

but it's her mind that really drives me wild.

Goals, ambitions so high,

my heart thrives to open up and try.

A new beginning that may not end,

she's got potential to be more than a friend.

With those pretty eyes

and classy smile,

this girl and I can hang out for a while.

Who's That Girl?

There's Something About You

There's something about you, I think about daily;

me falling in love, seemed oh so crazy.

My life had been shattered, heart torn and battered;

left with a feeling, that love didn't matter.

Then I met you, as gracious as a dove;

we both fit together, like a hand in a glove.

There's something about you, blowin my mind;

your inner most beauty, shows all the time.

There's something about you, I can't put into words;

but you make my heart sing, with your warmth and your love.

A beautiful melody that strums like a harp;

comforts my fears and caresses my heart.

There's something about you, that I really like;

your strength to ignite, my fears to flight.

There's something about you, I think about daily;

totally awesome, and driving me CRAZY!

Across the room

I couldn't help but notice you from across the room.

And I must say, your attractiveness does loom.

Do you come here often? Or a first time or two?

I don't normally approach strangers, but today,

    I'm trying something new.

Since you caught my eye from across the room,

I'm taking this chance for embarrassment and gloom.

Is there someone special, who's heart you do consume?

Because you're catching eyes here,

    as your allure beams across the room.

I would hope they understand, you stand out in a crowd,

You have a certain appeal and your confidence

    speaks clear and loud.

NO WORRIES, I'M SINGLE,

    AND THANKS FOR STOPPING BY.

TO BE QUITE FRANK AND HONEST,

    YOU ALSO CAUGHT MY EYE.

WITH ALL THESE PEOPLE HERE,

    YOU MADE MY OPTICS ZOOM.

YOUR FLAIR AND YOUR AURA,

    ALSO BEAMED ACROSS THE ROOM.

I'M ON MY WAY OUT AND RUNNING A BIT LATE,

PLEASE TAKE MY CARD,

    LET'S CHAT ABOUT A FUTURE DATE.

I'LL SEE YOU SOON, AM I ALLOWED TO ASSUME?

& I'M GLAD WE SPOTTED EACH OTHER,

        FROM

            ACROSS THE ROOM

Can A Man
Love His Woman?

Just as deep and hard

as a woman can love her man,

A man, can love his woman.

He can love her to the depths,

with everything he can.

A man, can love his woman.

With temptations, from all his adulations,

A man, can love his woman.

From their love's foundation, and throughout
their duration,

A man, can love his woman.

She becomes Ms. Everything, a joy to life she brings,

A man, wants this woman.

With a passion and zing, to let go of old things,

A man, loves this woman.

She's felt insecure and unsure, does he really love me?

Yes. A man, can love, his woman.

But a man

can't spend

24/7 saying

how much he loves,

But when a man loves his woman,

she feels reassured.

Even though at times, her man, can feel insecure and unsure himself.

When that man, really loves, that woman.

Real love is Hot! It's like hitting the jack pot!

Sometimes, many times, he can be afraid.

Fearful to lose, for what he's prayed.

Yes. A Man, Can Love His Woman.

Come to me

If you ever feel uneasy

Don't be afraid to come to me

I'll keep my mind open for you to come freely

Share your desires your pleasures your needs

Never run here or there to guess my feelings

Friends and family could guess, but not know really.

I never want you to have that wondering look

If you ever feel shaken or ever feel shook

Come to me with whatever jolted you,

Let's talk & look & close that book

I wish I could spend every moment making you feel
safeguarded

Reflect on where we are & remember where we started.

If your heart ever feels doubt

Don't ask my neighbors what I'm all about

They wouldn't know my heart; they wouldn't know my core.

Grab your phone, to talk text scream or shout

& Whatever it is Baby, together, we'll work it out.

Come to me with hurts and pains.

Come to me with stress and strains.

Come to me with your successes and your gains.

I have a shoulder for your tears your fears and old chains.

Together you and me, let's start a family.

& Baby Always, Come To Me

Falling in Love with You

Falling in Love with you is what my heart keeps wanting to do,

so quickly for you my feelings grew,

to adore and appreciate you.

Falling in Love is hard for me to do,

but you made me feel wanted and special,

every time I chatted with you.

True Love is a gift from the highest,

he chooses whom he chooses,

and, he's totally unbiased.

Falling in Love with you feels incredibly sweet!

Your caring and comfort

makes me feel complete.

Falling in Love is usually slow for me to do,

but without even a clue,

my heart keeps bringing me back to you.

Every minute of my day, you're all I think of,

I feel happy & Blessed, to be falling in love

I Always Loved You

I always loved you

      -the closest relationship to perfect, that I ever knew

I always loved you

      -we learned together, and we grew

Whether you believe it or not, I always loved you

      -I didn't realize, you were my Idealized Boo

But my heart was under lock and key,

      -before you broke through

      - no one since, has touched my heart like you

I always loved you

      - what we had was so darn special,

      -and I didn't have a clue

I always loved you

      -I never loved another, the same way that I loved you

Believe it or not, I always loved you

       -no matter what I did and no matter what I'll do

I'll always love you

       -my greatest blunder in life,

       -was not keeping you for life

I'll always love you

       -

       -

       -FOREVER

16

I'd rather do wrong

The first moment I met you, it was such a delight,
>   My heart skipped a beat, you were perfectly my type.
With my heart in my throat and a crack in my voice,
>   I said good morning, without thinking about Joyce.
The sexiness in your voice, took my breath away,
>   You almost left me speechless but I had plenty to say.
I wish I had met you earlier in life,
>   And I still want to know you, but I do have a wife.
Your magnetism, your flair, It brightens the light,
>>   At this moment in time, I'd rather do wrong,

than do right.

>   I'm attracted to you too, and can certainly follow the game plan,
>   If I can't see you when I want, I'll certainly see you when
>>   I can.
>   I will take you on the ride of your life, Mr. married man,
>   The only rule is, you can't fall in love, for as long as you
>>   can.

I'm so glad we met that day back in May,
>   And my feelings have grown, a little carried away.
>   You sweep me off my feet, every time our bodies meet,

17

With compatibility off the CHART, great mountain peaks feel bittersweet.

Maybe I'm wrong to keep holding on, to my Best SEX, Ever!

We travel to the moon and beyond, with each love making endeavor.

I don't want to do right if it means our travels are through,

I don't want to do right, if there's NO MORE MOON to See With You.

I didn't know an affair, could change one's sight,

But If loving you is wrong, I don't want to

see right.

My BLE (Best Lover Ever)

Instantaneously Flirting

Sharing a good thought instantaneously

-may capture attention, by the words that are mentioned.

Flirting a thought instantaneously

- may start to brew, something brand new.

Flirting out a thought instantaneously

-could set the stage to further engage.

You observe for a moment, and then you begin to gauge

- did the flirt that I made, put us on the same page.

Flirting a thought can be a nice way to greet

- It can be a surprising treat, and, accomplish a feat.

When you see someone Hott! Create words on the spot

-whether nervous or scared, give it what you got!

Instantaneously flirting with a cutie you see

- could make that person wonder, *are they feelin me?*

Instantaneously flirting, is common to do

   - Girls flirt, guys flirt, so, …do you?

Instantaneously Flirt?.

It's a beautiful thing, when it leads to a fling,

When consenting adults,
move on impulse.

Instantaneously.

Looking

Looking for someone who can capture the imagination
Someone who can capture my endearing adoration
Looking for someone who can infiltrate my heart
Someone whose words, connect from the start.

Looking for someone who stands out in the crowd
Someone who stands proud, while well-endowed
Looking for someone who stands confident,

not pretending, not loud

Someone open enough,

to soar naked with me

on a cloud?

Looking for something that my brain & past

won't sabotage
Looking for something I hope is attainable,

that's real, not a mirage.

Looking for someone who can add a laugh to my day
Someone who can add a smile, with a simple OK
Looking for someone who can add richness to my thoughts
Someone who can add debate,

To some ideologies I've Bought.

Looking for someone who can keep my attention
Looking for someone who's a keeper,

In every dimension

Looking for someone who keeps life,

Love and all things real
Looking for that lover

Willing to fight side by side,

When one turns ill.

Love Notes (Diary of my real love Journeys)

#1
Gm,
How are you feeling?
I thoroughly understood all of your words and I agree to support you & follow your lead!
I want you to be as Healthy and as Whole, As You Can Possibly Be...

#2

You're My Treasure Babe...

Allow me to Polish my Treasure & Make It Shine?

Can we wine and dine, until the end of time?

#3
I want to take you to the galaxies...
In more ways than one
Along the route we'll construct fresh memories and produce tons of fun.
Together there, we'll mingle with the Stars and flirt with the Moon
And every night we'll say goodnight...
to the warmth of the Sun with sweet memories to consume

#4

Yesterday you asked, "What changed?"

The answer is, I'm learning you more, day by day.

& I have an affinity to learn with a desire to be better... Change

And now when my eyes look upon you nothing looks quite the same.

Love Changes...

23

#5

By the way...

Every Man Has moments that

he needs his woman to help

him in Confidence

Just in case none have been

honest enough 2 say

Just Saying...

#6

Learning Ur Hot Spots

We've already taken great excursions together

While I still learn the many ways that will Excite U.

As U teach me those, we get 2 travel to the Moon & Beyond.

& Cuddle & Kiss & Feel Love as we Journey back

From the Milky Way together

#7

Sex without emotions & feeling = just sex

Sex with Emotions with the Person U Dig = Magical Moments

Magical Moments = Steps towards Love Making 🖤 🖤

Love Making 🖤 🖤 is what I Want With U

I know that we both turn down just Sex Opportunities...

#8

You can have sex from Lust

You can have Sex With Love

I choose LOVE & I choose you BABY

But I do Lust 4 Ur Love

Lustin My Baby's Lovin

#9

Babe

We make falling in love

So darn Hard!!

Because

We stay in our own way.

I'm falling for you

& I know

You're falling for me

But our minds just won't let us be

Our past history, Won't Set Us FREE

#10   Every time my phone dings, When I look at it, I want it to be a message from you. & When I see your name, my insides light up

#11

Kay decided RD is too busy 4 a partner & never told me she might b interested in a partner relationship & never talked 2 me about partnerships

But she figured Randall was too busy all her on her own

Hmmm...

& Randall is all into her

Lol

#12

Lol,

I don't want you to stay out of my way & I didn't ask you to

I want you in my world!!!

#13 **So**, how my mind is wired My Princess,

when you think that I send my special

messages to everyone I date

it makes me think that's what she

does but I don't DO THAT!

#14

Babe, why don't you say these things to me that you
allow to slip out from time to time?? Dialogue about
your Heart so I can know what's in your Heart...

#15

U have said little things to me

that makes me feel like Love 4 me is growing

in Ur heart

but you have never really opened up on US & Me

& If U see any vision on US long-term

(that always makes me feel like U want to keep searching)

Our past history, Won't Set Us FREE

27

Meeting You

Meeting you was a moment in time,

Although you left me dangling, you still stayed on my mind.

A splendid conversation & a bunch of sex appeal,

You uttered that you were married,

& that killed the deal.

Little to my surprise, you had a little more to convey,

I was shocked when you reached out to me,

on social media one day.

Totally perplexed &

not sure of your intent,

But you made my day that day by giving me consent.

To open the door & explore what you're all about,

Are you still married? Why did you reach out?

You explained that years had passed, since you sent that text,

But some way, somehow, I missed your text request.

Nevertheless, once I saw it, I put my mind & finger to task,

To finally send that request reply, to come to you at last.

You explained that you're still married, and that I was a threat,

You live a faithful Christian life, but your needs aren't being met.

Torn deep down inside, like a lion trapped in a cage,

Yearning for natural freedom, before the golden age.

Day by day, up and down, programmed by the beat of a drum,

Day by day, it's hope and pray, your spouse will help you cum?

Curiosity loomed, that day of Meeting You,

Living miles apart, but still our friendship grew.

Then it turned into Romance, after a Magical dance,

So glad you texted me, so glad you took a chance.

To explore the possibilities, to explore what may be there,

I'm thrilled I'm riding with you, on such a Glorious Love Affair.

We journeyed through the Milky Way, to places we never knew

I'm glad you captured my attention, the first day of Meeting You.

Ms. Queen,

I'm very thankful that I met you Beautiful Queen. Thanks for allowing me to enter your world to explore your scene. I do want to be clear; I do not live an abstinent life & I would prefer a Monogamous World. The way I MAKE LOVE AND GIVE LOVE I'm a throwback to Adam & Eve in the Garden. Exuberating Unadulterated Love Making with Liberty & Freedom for all!! The way I believe God Intended, splendid and extended.

But for Me, Finding That Special One U Can Dream To Grow Old With Is Absolutely Priceless!!! When the beauty fades and the aches and pains rage and the frailty of man begins to engage. Having someone by your side when a new illness arises, when the doctor advises, when a love one's death is made aware, and you're both there. You gradually age together, pushing wheelchairs, yet the love and loyalty is still there, that's my dream, my request, my Prayer.

Therefore, a King should determine to be fair, when he realizes, his Heart is not going there. Unfortunately, everything we start doesn't capture the Heart. Be smart to depart as friends, before an end where a friendship falls apart, without a mend. So instead of perpetually jerking a Queen around on a dead-end road, we should respect her value, her treasure and the love she showed.

I have a couple of friends, whom I purposefully give space to, not to cripple their wings anymore, so that they may again soar. Great Friends & Fantastic Women who gained a special place in my Heart but the love bug never bit me. Sometimes I've asked why, but I already knew the answer. The Heart is the Boss of the Love Gate!! It chooses whom it will let in & whom it will castrate. She could have been beautiful, smart, hand-picked, and damn near perfect! But often times, man nor woman has total control of their Heart. The Heart can be fickle and control thoughts unaligned with your mind. Sometime the Heart makes you Love, when you don't want to love... Painful love can tug at your Heart and tug at your Heart and tug at your Heart. The Heart can be complex & tricky & Heartache can be confusing & sticky. So, it does pain my Heart, 2 walk away from pieces of my Heart, & hope they Soar High & Bright, be it without me. But Fairness Rules! It's probably only a very tiny-tiny amount of selfishness in this body and these bones.

Life is so short, live life fair and live life keen!!! Be true to ourselves, and let's talk truth my Dear Queen. We've done what we've done, we've seen what we've seen. Let's remove our masks, our fictitious smokescreens.

Ms. Beautiful Queen, let's convene in some jeans,
Pure open and honest dialogue, Ms. Beautiful Queen!!

my new Man

I got a new man, he's charming and sweet,

My new man is so wonderful, he even massages my feet!

He cooks me breakfast in bed & then, he makes the bed,

Whenever he gets down, he makes an awesome spread.

He knows just what I like, the right season and the right spice,

I can't figure out how, he's always concise

My new Man keeps passing my test,

This guy appears to be different from the rest.

He likes the things I like, making love thru the night,

Then keep our bodies' tight, exercise at first light.

In business we're alike, we're both very shrewd

This new Man I'm claiming, can I find him in you?

32

November 22

It was kind of interesting. I was into my own world, not actively looking to meet someone new. Then on that day, I met someone with a Lovely Smile, that had a Pretty Face too. I was Instantly Attracted but thought it's probably better to keep My World as is. My plate was already full with friends. But 4 some reason, after that initial meeting, I kept seeing that Lovely Smile, & that Pretty Face with flair & grace. She finally cornered me one day & said, "we have to have a Face2Face conversation." I'm So Thankful She did, because @ that Face2Face I got to Learn that the Pretty Face with the Lovely Smile, was a Beautiful Woman, that was perfectly, my style. I'm a fast learner so it didn't take long to see, this Beautiful Person, was Just Right 4 me.

That day in November, I'll always remember, I saw U & U looked So Gorgeous 2 me, that day U surpassed being Beautiful, as far as my eyes could see. Gorgeous is a word I use very seldom because for me it's a combination of Pretty-ness, Beauty, Style, Grace & Character. At that moment moving forward, I saw glimpses of your Gorgeous Beauty, I had yet 2 meet. U quickly became Special in My Heart, in a way that makes Me Melt, U touched the inner fibers of Me, in a way

I Never Felt.

Randall Daniels

Once Upon A Time

Have you ever wanted to love again?

But didn't know how?

Ever been reluctant to date,

Because scars from a previous vow?

Ever met someone unexpectedly,

That gave you reason for pause?

But all your experiences collectedly,

Has Cemented Your Jaws.

From expressing a slight Wow of delight,

Because U feel within, U can't do LOVE right.

Intrigued by the words they shared,

Their conversation made U aware,

Their passion for people, articulated they care,

Let's fight 4 all, 2 be treated fair.

Inner beauty on full display,

& your eyes are happy too.

Perhaps the package you been waiting 4,

Finally Arrived 2 You!

BUT this love thing U tried, Again & Again…

Now it's something YOU just won't allow!

Tho moments & days, You Wish LOVE Again,

But U say to yourself, *I don't know how.*

Sprinkle hope with faith once again my friend,

When 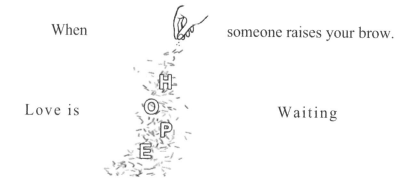 someone raises your brow.

Love is   Waiting

4 A n o t h e r   C h a n c e .

W a i t i n g ,

TO SHOW YOU HOW...

W A I T I N G

The Fear of Love

For an era in time, I've been afraid to love

Discarded by a lover I once fought to love

Now alone I stand on this beautiful night

And at this very moment in time, I feel solitary in life

Watching the blissful moon cuddle the star filled sky

My body keeps craving for your magical high, anxious for your lovin to arrive

Something wonderful is coming over me

I'm essentially processing you and me, continually

Once love deprived but now I feel alive

With every touch of love, that penetrates deep down inside

Your terrific touch, is the sensation I need

It comforts me, then let's love proceed

I'm ready for love, truly willing to love

Fearfully pushed the fear of love aside

Allowing new thoughts to engage my mind

Now I feel the need to feel your flesh

Pressed close to mine

Your love has been amazingly engaging from the start

Your love then, infiltrated my heart

Glad my heart finally opened, to feel love again

Fearful from where I've been,

Fearful to pull out love, buried deep within

I love your love, your sweet sweet love

And I'm ready for lovin, right now

Cum over, like now!

My love was lost in the lost and found

But now, I'm genuinely loving your lovin,

and I want your lovin, right now!

A Glimpse of Beauty

A **G**limpse of **B**eauty
   is what you have given me
My hope is that what's inside you
   will match the outside beauty I see
Only You & God know the reason
   You chose me to befriend
A world filled with so many people
   why allow me to come in?
Your stunning beauty will have appeal
   To men & women worldwide

   Your charming grace will give a cowardly person
   A heart big enough inside
   To embrace **G**limpses of **B**eauty
   God Blessed you to endow
   Your smile, your eyes, your style
   And certainly, your WOW!!
   Maybe one day we both can say
   that we met a cutie
   The cutie we met had the biggest heart
   And that cutie, shared, a **G**limpse of **B**eauty!

TRIPLE BLACK

I stepped in a club debonair and chic,

Sporting fitted clothes, detailing my physique.

My profile was low, dressed in triple black,

The hottest lady I saw, I kept her face to my back.

This woman I seek, kept trying to peek,

At the brother in black, looking strong, yet meek.

I finally gave her a glance; she gave a nod and a wink,

Guys looking jealous because they're buying her drinks.

She stopped by my table & gave her business card

& Said:

"I'm the woman you want, why you playin me this hard?

I've only seen your profile but I like your triple black,

But can your ambitions and dreams,

Bring a lady back?"

40

Hmm, my appeal for her took flight & ascension,

Her very clever question, captured my attention.

My profile stayed smooth in my triple black,

I first ordered her a bottle, of Top-Shelf Cognac,

While already ready, for my smooth comeback.

"Yes,

I make it a practice

To bring the ladies back.

I'm the man you want.

The debonair hustler.

Sporting Triple Black."

True Love

True love, true love, you waited so long.

To introduce yourself to me and make my heart your home.

You continually waited, though fond memories I knew,

Which made me wonder, is such a thing true?

I heard fabulous stories of the delight you bring,

Joy that stimulates, like the first day of spring.

I heard you leave an aroma that can't be out done,

Sweeter than scents of flowers and candles, all rolled into one.

True love you're a jewel as priceless as time,

I hear if nurtured properly, like time you will chime.

True love you crept in through a friend, who I appreciate,

To come through someone so special, was well worth the wait.

True love, one question, *"Will you meet, everyone?"*

You bring plenty smiles and make life, much more fun.

Gorgeous as the sunset, as beautiful as a dove,

It's been a pleasure to meet you, TRUE LOVE, TRUE LOVE

Valerie

The definition of Valerie, means stunning and beautiful,

I didn't know that definition when I met you but I would add

wonderful,

Smart beautiful nostalgic and graceful.

You are everything that I could hope for in a mate.

I never experienced love at first sight, I use to think it was fake,

But my love begun brewing, on our very first date.

Valerie, you allowed me to experience love in a way I never had

before.

I thought of your smile your eyes your character, the moment my

feet hit the floor.

If I could squeeze 28 hours in a day, I would think of you even

more.

A beautiful diamond in the rough, that made my heart throb

galore.

In such a short amount of time I was compelled to cut all other

loose ends,

I was upfront and honest that I wasn't monogamist, and I had

friends.

One by one I called and shared my news,

To stoic voices, not remotely amused.

You were a love song to my heart, that gave me hope each day,

And every day that I saw you, you took my breath away.

No matter your endeavor and no matter with whomever,

No matter what our reason was, I will love you forever.

I reflect on us many a day, the essence of you will never decay.

With all my love tries, I never knew my heart would fall this way,

I fight to hide it baby, but at times my feelings won't obey.

Everyone should be Blessed to feel love this way, real love, not for show or for play.

If you should ever need me, just send a message, and I'll follow the star

No matter where you are, no matter how far, I will get there by plane train or car.

Since you decided on a new direction, I keep my feelings, surfaced below.

But my love is still alive and only needs a call from you to grow.

I'm not mad or sad but happy for you, and hope you're made complete.

Whoever the lucky lad is, has the Best Woman he'll ever meet.

I may not have expressed the depth of the love I feel for you,

And I regret that, it contributed to me losing you.

I thought I fully expressed the love and admiration I have for you.

The things you say that tore us apart, left me quite perplexed and feeling blue.

Now water under a bridge, I want you successful and your life to thrive.

Such a talented person, you have more gifts than you realize.

I'll always cherish meeting you and the memories we made.

In time my pain will subside and in time the love will fade.

My Magic Moments with you were shortened and stolen,

But I would do it all over again, if even for a moment.

In life, we can't control the things we can't control.

I wanted you for life and that was out of my control.

Ms. Valerie.

You were one of the best things
 to happen to me this lifetime,
So, no matter where life takes us,
you will always have a rhythmic beat in my heart,

That periodically chimes, for our unforgettable times.

Love You For Life!

Ms. Valerie

When You
Love Someone

When you Love Someone perhaps you react a little unusual,

  -you don't realize it, but you don't keep living life, same as usual.

Reactions become different but the overall person is the same,

  -when love in your heart grows, the game begins to change.

When you Love Someone and it's not a manufactured love,

  -many steps along the way, you discover things to dispose of.

There's a divine joy and an overwhelming bliss,

  -Always ready to erupt & explode with every enchanted kiss.

Pure love & thoughts keep your smile in place,

  -Walking on cloud nine the times you're not floating in space.

Finding someone to cherish and hope to spend the rest of your days with is a gift,

  -thinking these opportunities always come around, a gamble & myth.

Absolute admiration, tranquility and praise from your lover,

  -has the ability to strengthen fragility, just allow them to uncover,

Your scars, your hurts, your doubts, your fears,

  -pains, locked & sealed by years & years, & countless tears.

When you Love Someone, it becomes a brand-new day,

  -old friends and companions are now put away.

When you Love Someone and your love is pure,

  -you'll examine your heart to make sure you're sure.

When you Love Someone there's no need to delay,

  -you hold on tight with all your might and don't give way.

When you Love Someone, life adds new excitement and fun,

  -you have a passion to see them happy…

When You

Love Someone

Work of Art

Mona Lisa,

a *w*ork *of a*rt,

Every room you're in,

your beauty is set apart.

A stunning centerpiece,

I would never lease,

Exquisite head turner,

A Picturesque Show Piece!

Your leering vibe is so alive,

With a sex appeal that doesn't deprive.

Eye candy, with a beautiful split,

I know that you know, You're Killin It!!

48

How do I take you home?

Fly you to Manhattan? Fly you to Rome?

You're beautiful, and the piano is having all the fun,

You're the artistry I've been looking for, you're the one!

Mona Lisa, travel with me?

Let's sail the seven seas.

A new journey, let's create a memory.

We'll ride and ride,

And when the ride stops, we'll lay side by side.

You caught my eye from the very start.

After my very first glance,

I inquired about this Masterful,

<u>W</u>ork <u>O</u>f <u>A</u>rt

When I gaze at the moon
and see the stars,
I think of how
we've come so far.

You Are Everything

You're a long-sought treasure
that tingles my spine,
A treasure looked for but many won't find.
You adorn my space every time you're present,
You've acquired a knack to make everything pleasant.
You are everything, and everything is you,
My innermost feelings inside, I wish you only knew.
And if you really knew, so often next to you,
My body somersaults, a real-life dream come true.
I'm so glad I met you, you stay on my mind,
From the very first day, our hearts have aligned.
With difficulties and hard times, we always mend,
Friends that ascend, we'll ride & die til the very end.
You are my everything, from apple pie to a diamond ring.
Simply what you are, a gift that can't be beat,
My everything, you make my world complete.

50

You Looked

The first time I saw you, I was nervous and shook,

-But I kept looking at you, and I hoped, that you

looked.

You caught my attention as you passed my way,

-that body, that face, what else can I say?

Your charming Beauty gave me a jolt,

- you looked loose and free like an unbridled colt.

Looking stunning, looking cunning, you looked like

mine,

-I was predicting the future, hoping the stars

would align.

51

You're well put together, like classical jazz,

- Smooth swag, classy class, & to top it off, Crazy

Pizazz!

Something in your smile, I saw as key,

- Your smile plus the slight tilt of your head,

-said, you're coming on to me.

Your overall look I can't put in words,

-but to sum it all up,

-you make my speech slurred!!

Your smile always greets me at the top of my day,

A smile that seems to say, today is your day.

Your smile is so lovely it even glows in the light,

A radiant smile that makes a dreary day bright.

Your smile seems to subtly, command my attention,

A smile that's pure, innocent and stays while you listen,

Your smile makes me smile, and makes my heart weak,

An essence of beauty, that's long in mystique.

I think your smile is refreshingly pleasant;

It lingers around even when you're not present.

Your picturesque smile is heaven sent;

   A tranquil power, that's no accident.

Your smile, your smile, it's fully equipped,

   Such nice-looking teeth and soft looking
lips.

Your smile, your smile, makes my heart grow fond,

   It gives warmth when I see it and makes our

      friendship bond.

Thoughts of your smile

   and beauty stay for a while,

      I'm guilty of daydreaming, just thinking about

YOUR SMILE.

ICE BREAKER

I'm Regretful Pop

Pops man, I'm regretful,
And I'm fretful.
The hurt I caused,
Put our relationship on pause.
Years since we spoke,
Learned about your stroke.
Mom told me,
You said, "let him be."
Mom said you're still sick,
But don't want to see me.

You were usually right,
And I left in spite.
You're a good man Dad,
Your Son was mad.
Mad I didn't
See you more.
Mad I saw other dads
And kids having fun galore.
Mad at how
You treated Mom.
You missed all my things,
Including my prom.
But it wasn't just you,
I was mad at the world.

I'm regretful Pop,
I couldn't stop.
Being angry
Got the best of me.
My errors can't be undone,
but will you please see me?
Your Son...

Ice Breaker

From the moment I saw you, you had such an appeal,

Your charisma and charm appeared genuine and real.

A splendid smile with perfectly shaped lips,

That simply melted my heart and made my insides flip.

Fearful to approach you, I didn't know what to say,

I sent a shout out to God, to send you my way.

Perhaps he didn't get my message, because you turned and walked away,

I chose to embarrass myself to meet you, because I only have today.

I was checking you out and I observed,

You don't wear a ring, so I got up this nerve.

You appear to be friendly, I watched you smile with everything that you do,

I'm curious to know you, because your inner beauty shines through.

I promise I'm not crazy or lazy, I'm a mover and a shaker,

Nervous with my own words,

so, I employed this *Ice Breaker.*

Ice Breaker 2

Hello, I've seen you around a few times before,

I tried to say hi one day, as we passed by the door.

You appeared to be hurrying, so I couldn't get your attention,

You always look nice, and that's what I wanted to mention.

I like the sports gear you wear; you appear to be active,

You're killing that outfit today, you're very attractive.

If you don't mind me asking, what's your name?

Friends and FAM call me _____, do you have a nickname?

My nickname is reserved, for people who are close,

I'm sharing it with you now, in preparation and in hope.

That one day we'll find the magic, and our chemistry gets us hooked,

I bet your personality, will outlast your darn good looks.

I'm actually quite nervous to be speaking with you right now,

I got up this courage and I don't even know how

For this more reserved person to be out on a limb,

I'm very attracted to you, so I approached on a whim.

These words caught my attention on a piece of paper,

And they gave me courage to share as an *Ice Breaker.*

I'm Your Momma

Girl you know I'm your Momma,
And I can stir up some drama.
I've said hurtful things to you,
I'd just be in a mood.
But I'm still your Momma,
And I love you.
When you had Daddy trauma,
I should have come through

.

I tried to be a good Mom,
But we learn as we go.
I messed up so many times,
More than you know.
But my greatest mistake of all,
Was not giving you a call.
I let so much time go by,
Stubbornness, and I didn't reply.

Always thought I was supposed to be in charge,
So, I let our disagreement get too large.
I want to talk, see what you have brewing,
I need to hear your voice, know how my Daughter is doing.
I miss you dearly,
That's from Momma's heart, sincerely.

My Father's Day Post

Post Written By: Brittian Daniels, My Son

Britt Daniels

I've been writing this post since Father's Day.

When I was growing up we grew up in an Apostolic deliverance ministry. We were big on power and demonstration, but also teaching. We were taught dealing with demonic activity to be careful, because spirits transfer. We were also taught homosexual was a spirit.

As a teenager my dad did what he felt was right to protect my family based on the teaching we were taught. And I was no longer able to live there. The truth of the matter is once upon a time my dad wasn't my hero, but the villain in my story.

What I'm soooooooo grateful for today is that's not how things stayed. We talked daily. Take road trips. He's my therapist when it comes to relationships. He swoops in when I need something fixed on my car. He hangs with my friends like they're his own kids. We pray and study the Word together. My dad is my super hero!!!

I want to encourage some of you all with similar stories to simply forgive. Our parents did the best they could, and what they thought was right based on what they knew. People grow, mature, change, and develop over time. Just like you. You aren't the same person you were 5 years ago either. You may discover the person they are become is the hero you've always wanted.

Dad I love you man! Happy Father's Day!!!

6/22/2021 at 3:48 PM

Britt Daniels

My Father's Day post. Wanted to make sure you were good with it first.

/22/2021 at 3:49 PM

Thanks for sharing first, & I'm cool with it. Makes me teary-eyed

Britt Daniels   6/22/2021 at 4:05 PM

I love you frfr! 💯💪

6/22/2021 at 4:05 PM

Love U2 Son!!
2 Infinity & further

6/22/2021 at 4:06 PM

Posted June 22, 2021

Brittian Getting his Dad

prepared for a Photo Shoot.

May 31, 2021

Son teaching Dad @ Photo Shoot

Excited to be bonding......

62

Selfish

I've been selfish, living life about me
I always get caught up,
every time I think I'll be free.
You have every right to be hurt,
I spent life chasing skirts.
Always on the go,
without you in my vision,
I made bad decision
after bad decision.
Lived what I learned,
from the men I looked up to,
Sow your wild oats, what they said do.

I had an egotistical disorder in my mind,
I felt that every pretty woman I wanted,
was supposed to be mine.
There are no excuses, nothing can justify,
I wish I was a better father, a better ally.

We haven't spoken in a while,
I don't know if you'll
let me reconcile.
I'm trying to reach out,
and I'm nervous.
Because,
I gave you a history,
of lip service.
God has allowed me to get older and wiser somehow,
And I value things a little differently now.

If you please reply to me, I would love to hear from
you.
For me this is brand new, I hope for a chance to be a
different father,
than who you once knew.

Signed, *Unselfish Now*

64

Whatever I did

Hello there, how are you doing?

I'm reaching out to you, in hopes of undoing.

Whatever we did wrong, it's been too long,

I love you too much, to let this prolong.

I don't even remember what tore us apart,

We were closer than siblings from the very start.

Best friends, like peas in a pod,

When people saw us apart, they thought that was odd.

Please forgive me for whatever I did,

Our friendship got bottled up, and I want to remove this lid.

I want to grow old & go to my grave,

Knowing in my heart, my best shot I gave.

Our friendship, an insane ride and great endeavor,

I'm fighting now, not to let it end forever.

I love you and all your quirky ways,

Please accept my quirkiness, and friendship, for the rest of our days?

Why?

I have a question that's perplexing to me,
It pops in my head sporadically.
Whether I'm busy or relaxing under a tree,
I've asked myself over and over, why me?

The question I have is scary you see,
I've laid awake many nights wondering; did it have to be?
Did you love me? Did you give me up for a fee?
Why not the others? Why just me?

You gave me up for adoption,
Did you see worth in me? Was that your only option?
Most of my life, I've been afraid you may reject or deny,
But I'm strong enough now, to ask my question, why?

Why did you leave me at birth?
Did you not see my potential once I entered earth?
I was raised with care and love, as life flew by,
But it wasn't with you, are you comfortable enough to answer... Why?

MOTIVATIONAL
POEMS

mbition

Ambition,

A desire to achieve success.

Ambition is,

An innate yearning, to be your best.

Ambition should be the epitome,

To BE AS SUCCESSFUL AS YOU CAN BE!!

You can continue to watch the rich get richer in your face,

Or you can get in the game, carve out your niche in this place.

Ambition that's inside YOU, wants you to Envision,

Million-Dollar homes, come from Million-Dollar Visions.

Keep moving forward with courage,

to change your condition.

True Pursuit Is Priceless.

AND THEY CALL IT...

*A*mbition

I GET IT, The life WE were dealt is Hard & Unfair

Sympathy is comforting

And makes lifes un-fairness easier to bare.

The hand WE were dealt, was dealt.

How WE play our hand determines

How high WE will Soar,

How loud WE will Roar!

And Where WE Land,

Our Destiny Still Resides...

In Our Very Hands

S-O-A-R!!

10,000 HOURS

One of the greatest feelings in the world,

is being on top of your game

Being on top of their game has propelled some

to Stardom, Wealth, and Fame

How do you get there, rising to the top?

Some say Put In 10,000 hours,

some Say NEVER STOP

Some scholars say 10,000 hours of practice

creates Mastery

Some debate that theory, like it's blasphemy

I'll Chase 10,000 hours feeling great or with a cough

My motto is…,

"No Days Off!!"

In 10,000 hours for many,

Mastery Came.

So, following a blueprint of success,

is no need for shame

Things built from the same blueprint will mirror,

and look the same

And one of the greatest fulfillments you can claim,

is Being On TOP!

No Matter Your Game

2 hours

2 hours seem like an eternity, 2 a child,

2 hours can make a child feel alone, even exiled.

2 hours can change a child's mind and perception,

2 hours is enough time 2 make a child lose their dreams, by deception.

2 hours is enough time, 2 mentor a young mind,

2 hours is enough time 2 unwind, then find time.

2 hours can be the difference, between life and death,

2 hours can give a child hope, for another breath.

2 hours can erase ambitions 2 go get great,

2 hours can provide time, for a life altering mistake.

2 hours can be destructive for an idle mind,

2 hours can take open opportunities, 2 offer a mind, a life of crime.

2 hours is plenty fine, 2 volunteer some time,

Check homework, listen to a hurt, or say a silly rhyme.

You don't have 2 be perfect, it's impossible to do,

But just 2 hours of your time, for you 2 be, perfectly you.

AFL (Athlete For Life)

Great news!! If you   Never Ever

Played A

Sport,

  YOU Still

   Qualify!!

Being great as an athlete

is what God gifted me,

And no.

    He didn't give me

      super quickness

        and great strength you see.

He gave me the **mindset,**

    to be as great

      as I can be,

God gave me what I needed,

    the rest

      WAS UP TO ME.

Living a life with sports

is a fabulous life,

Getting paid to do

what you like,

there's not much better at life.

We get older and have kids,

then move on with life,

Because someone told us,

we can't be athletes for life.

I decided to differ with that,

And I encourage all,

get your mojo back.

Whether you're young or old, let's change and
commit,

To living healthy and fit,

your mind and body

will love you for it.

Life settles in, we stop physical activity cold

turkey,

but

trust

me,

your body can

still get

tight and perky.

You can walk through the mall or ride a bike at the park,

Hit a gym before dawn or jog in the dark.

Being an Athlete For Life, is only a **mindset,**

Just getting started, can be a first step to success.

Make A-F-L your new mantra, and your mind and body will win.

You'll begin to flaunt with confidence, because of the work you've put in.

Confidence Is A Lovely THING!!

Do it for your heart, do it for your mind,

Do it for that new spouse you're hoping to find.

Do it for your health, do it to refine.

Just do it

For all the benefits combined!

You will find it Fruitful,

Plus

Feel more Youthful,

BE, WHO YOU CAN SEE

IF YOU BELIEVE = YOU CAN ACHIEVE

REACH ANY HEIGHT, WITH VISION & FORESIGHT

BELIEVE IN YOU. MAKE YOUR DREAM COME TRUE.

YOU CAN BE, WHO YOU CAN SEE!

Business Deal

Here's the real on the business deal.

Making money is a TREMENDOUS Thrill!

And a Thrill so Real, will convince some to steal,

So many times Greed, sabotaged, the deal.

WIN-WIN relationships always last longer,

Winning together, make relationships stronger.

No need to be unfair, steal & cheat,

Living the Ugly Life of Beat, or Get Beat!

It's not a fun life, with no trust you can feel.

So always Remember, make it WIN-WIN,

WHEN

MAKING A DEAL!

Confidence Is A Funny Thing

The Greatest Achievers

Will Struggle

With Confidence

Because the mind

A fickle place

Given consecutive rejections

Confidence

Becomes misplaced

Confidence grows

With preparedness

In any Craft

Let's Be Clear

The **GREATEST COMPETITOR**

Gunning **4 Y**ou

Lives **B**etween **Y**our **E**ars

YOUR MIND

Every Ounce

I gave every ounce

That you can have some bounce

Exerted every muscle fiber

Your #1 fan, I'm a subscriber

Then one day you walked away

Many hours of work, you gave away

Your greatness is near, not far away

I didn't understand, how you could walk away

You dreamed and you strived

For your magic moment to arrive

You developed your talent

Your pursuit for success was noble and gallant

You had it all going

Your talent was growing

I helped you exalt

Then you put on the brakes, decided to halt

Breaking a parent's heart

Can tear them apart

They sacrifice their dreams with all their giving

For you a chance, at a better living

Consider heartbreaks too

When people bet on you

They see your potential

And their sacrifice is confidential

They miss paying a bill

For your dream to fulfill

They miss romance and dates

Because your success is at stake

Before you walk away

Consider if you stay

Consider if you achieve

The Greatness you believe

Consider how life will be

For your parents to cheer in glee

They sacrificed with you

To make   your dream come true.

When a lion sees   an opportunity to pounce,

They commit   with Every Ounce

When a Lion chance arises,

with **Every Muscle Fiber They Pounce**

Live with a heart of a King,

& **Pounce! With**

Every Ounce!!

Focusing Brilliantly

 In life, learn to work smarter, not harder!

Hunger for success, fun can rest some!

A total Sex and Fun paradigm,

Kills too much time!

Focus your quest, go relentless **Being Your Best!**

Get crispy and pearly by starting early!

AND It's never too late, **To Go Get** *Great!*

Learn Brilliancy, by Focusing Brilliantly!

Change your old days,

With Brilliant New Ways!

Future Millionaires

Future Millionaires... Who, Us?

-Yes Us, Millionaires, with surplus.

Us is a word I'm claiming to be,

-a word to describe, you and me.

With rhythmic hearts on a perpetual beat,

-hearts filled with courage, wanting to compete.

Challenging the world, the economy,

-this can be Us, but We gotta believe.

Always ask Yourself, who are You striving to be?

-break the curse of generations, stuck in poverty.

We got the guts, We got the heart,

-It's time We start perfecting our crafts, producing our own art.

A Millionaire Future Is Just A Dream Away,

-Let's get after it, don't miss a day.

The ones that focus the best, pass the rest,

-Discipline & Drive, a couple of keys
for Our success.

Missteps and blunders,

everyone has their share.

-Our shares can fuel us,

and produce

Future Millionaires...

I Lost, But I Gained

Each and every time I lost, it left a measure of pain

But the pain didn't reign, instead, it prompted
Change

Change, like becoming a better me

Change, the procrastinative person, I used to be

When I lost, I still Gained

Lived embarrassed riding the bench an entire
Basketball season

it fueled a player

To travel Europe playing b-ball

For MANY seasons

You see,

I lost, but I Gained

I lost in business so many times
But each time
I Gained knowledge,
on how to be Sharper on my grind
I lost, but I Gained

I was a slow reader in high school,
slow to retain
But I started rappin on a microphone,
and that all changed
I lost, but I Gained

Lost my marriage to divorce
Then God enrolled me
In his
Humble Persons Course
I lost, but still, I Gained

I wasn't smart enough

To marry my teenage

Sweetheart

But the daughter she gave me

Is Beautiful,

And packed with smarts

I've lost over and over again,

But I've Gained,

over and over and over and over...

Something that make us wonder,

Is a very small word called

IF

Perhaps

IF

I try that,

Or perhaps

IF

I do this.

Perhaps I'll sail the seven seas, or rap on a microphone;

IF

I push my mind to achieve, I can invent the unknown.

Perhaps I'll be a millionaire,

IF

only my mind will take me there;

My dreams can become very real for me, but only,

IF

I dare.

IF

you believe, you can achieve,

IF

you stay,

IF

you pray;

IF

you push your mind, your greatest tool,

IF

you shape it wise in school.

IF

is a Word very Small in Stature,

yet it Carries a Lot of Weight;

IF

a word that no matter what,

it will determine your fate.

IF

you want success, stay focused, don't
get blurred;

IF

can bring success, and it's just a
two-letter word.

IF

you let those special dreams die,

a part of you dies too;

IF

you strive and believe in your dreams,

IF

can power you through.

ME TOO

#METOO

I'm Sorry Bro, I didn't kno

I'm sorry to hear the words I just heard

A young lad around a man, whose vision was blurred

Men do unimaginable things to young boys

Then silence their mouths with fear fright and toys

It puts a lump in my throat and anger in my heart

To learn you had to carry something, so deep, and so dark

I just learned the fellows and I were your form of support

But none of us knew,

we would have gotten him to court

We went separate ways when High School was done

Your support system broken; the nightmares begun

Pain had been blocked by your mind, but there still
was a crime

Robbery of innocence, and the horror, can erupt at
anytime

Although this happened, a long time ago

I'm here with both ears. And I'm sorry Bro, I didn't
KNO

Friends for life…

NO FATHER NO

"NO FATHER NO!" The young chap yelled, under the billow,

With tears in his eyes the youngster cried, that night on his pillow.

Confused and unnerved, a different lad observed,

Some spiritual leader's actions, were a little perturbed.

Baffled and sad a new fella told his Dad,

About what happened to him and the ordeal he had.

Dad had a look on his face, as if he knew,

About the Church, these Priest, the many, not the few.

NO FATHER NO

The new fella never went back, but he never forgot,

About the day he was touched, in an uncomfortable
spot.

Some years later, visiting his Grandmother and
looking at her pearls,

She looked at him with a tear in her eye, and said,
they also do it to girls.

The new fella made a plea from that day on,

To be a voice for Grandmother, and all the voiceless
pawns.

NO FATHER NO

From teenager to adulthood the new fella understood,

Sexual misconduct and harassment should be fought
at statehood.

The new fella is a new father, a happily married man,

A new Politician, giving voice for the voiceless, as
best he can.

Boys still turn to men, that's been abused by
someone they knew,

It's refreshing to see we have men not afraid to say,
hashtag # ME TOO.

Trying To Get Home

Trying to get home before it was dark,

Because Grandmother is waiting,

with her harsh remarks.

On this nice breezy day, I took a shortcut through the field,

A quicker way home, is what it would yield.

On my quest, doing my best to beat the street lights,

I kept hearing noises but nothings in sight.

Getting more cautious before I proceed,

I turned around to look, and only saw long weeds.

I walked a little further but I kept hearing sounds,

But there was no one there, every time I turned around.

Trying To Get Home before it was dark,

This day things changed, & forever left a mark.

I didn't make it home before dark that day,

I didn't hear Grandmother's words to say.

This precious angel woke up in the hospital,

Nervous, fragile, scared and brittle.

Innocence and purity taken away,

With doctors explaining my ordeal, day by day.

A child molested and left to die,

But I'm a grown survivor, with grandkids,

loving Nana's pie.

Trying to get home, I was once a little child like you,

Now I've joined voices with the many women,

willing to say,

Me Too!

Uncomfortable

Uncomfortable at church, uncomfortable at work,

Working with guys that are perverted jerks.

Working in a field dominated by men,

Hearing sexual innuendos, again and again.

Outworking the men for my every promotion,

Afraid of demotion, I live with their, uncomfortable notions.

Church is a place you should feel safe and secure,

Men using uncomfortable tactics, trying to allure.

I justify why I don't stand up for myself,

The men have the power to put my career on the shelf.

This uncomfortable world, in which I'm forced to live,

We've been taught to look past and even forgive.

My friend keeps saying, if you let things be,

Who else out there, will stand up for me?

Cautious to tell my Pastor about the guys,

Because he stares with his eyes, and I'm afraid he may also surprise.

Now I'm more courageous to challenge their ways,

If repercussions come, I'll be prepared for those days.

I appreciate my friend's advice, he kept speaking the truth.

He said, think about the youth, and that gave me my boost.

No more silence, young women going through what I went through,

I've now joined the fight, hashtag, Me Too!

Every man

should take a stand,

&

support US women,

the best he can.

INSPIRING POETRY

Look in the mirror

Remember who you are
and stop falling asleep,
Look in the mirror,
and look really deep.
Get your motivation back
and stop living in lack,
You're not a punk
not weak,
so, stop acting like that.
Sleeping on your kids,
your career,
your future too,
We've all been down,
but you get up
& Fight Like the person You knew.

YOU

THE

PERSON I

KNEW

Don't just concede
 since you've been kneed in the gut,
  Life beat you down,
   and you can't get up??

Remember what Grandma
       & Pops taught?
             Reflect, Reminisce,
Look in the mirror
       Son, Look in the mirror
             Daughter,

You're better than this.
       You were taught how to **THRIVE**,
          NOT JUST SURVIVE,
       You have DNA in you,
          Different From Everyone Else Alive.

Look in the mirror,
       LOOK REAL HARD,
Someone gave their all for you,
       with their sweat and their scars.
For you to have better,
       a brighter future less marred.

          Look in the mirror,
          See Who You Are
          Look **Real DEEP**,
          Look **REAL HARD**...

Love Life!

God made me, to be me,

If he had made me any different,

only God knows, who I'd be.

With all of my imperfections and all of my strife,

Every day I smile, because I still Love Life.

When you feel good about yourself,

deep down inside,

When your world is crumbling, you can take it in stride.

A cheating husband or a cheating wife,

When you're good on the inside, you can still smile,
and Love Life

Being happy within yourself, can make you smile,

make you sing,

Always excited about the possibilities,

the next day will bring.

When your car is down and out of commission

as they say,

But you're so focused on you, your vehicle can't
stop,

a Great Great Day!

108

Understand your value

know your net worth,

God gave you exclusive DNA, for your birth to earth.

Your DNA is so rare,

it's worth a

heck of a price,

Love Life you rare jewel, your spice is twice as

NICE!

Meet failure with new plans

Most people will meet failure

some people stay in failure because their

lack of persistence

in creating new plans to take the place of

those which fail

If you fail to Plan, GUESS What??

You have planned,

You have planned to fail!!

SO

Meet failure with new plans,

Replace plans that can't, with plans that

can

One speed

GREATNESS

Live life engaged to be great,

Dream to get added to the Forbes wealthiest debate.

Everyone is given ambitions and desires,

Like LBJ and MLK but inspire to go higher.

The dreams you're given may better the earth,

Keep the imagination you were given at birth,

Learn to discover, what your dreams can be worth.

Life will knock you down,

　　　trying to get you to concede,

　　　　　Saying you can't be special,

　　　　　　　but keep fighting in One Speed.

Your speed of greatness,

is your speed to live by,

The greatness that's in you,

life fights to make it die.

When life knocks you down,

get up off your knees,

Remember who you are,

& Re-Capture Your Greatness Speed.

Pathway to Success

You must be mentally prepared to fail

In order to succeed

Failures, are the Pathway to Success

If we LEARN from the experiences

$$ EARNED $$

I have a friend in pursuit of her **PHD**

-She's gorgeous, brilliant, & soon, a Doctor she will be.

She said there's great stress because no moments are free

-I said, "Figure out how to un-stress, and go get that degree."

You remember in Junior High School, we had dreams without schemes?

-Now by any means, create schemes to propel your dreams.

A **PHD** is coveted, by companies worldwide

-Add that frame to your wall, show the world, You've Arrived!

Be like strong men and women who climbed that mountain of glee

-Letting go of non-supporting friends,

To Be The Best YOU Can Be.

Your **PHD** can bring dollars most people won't obtain

-Use that frame to start your campaigns, for the money you'll attain.

115

Tell the world, my name is in this frame and I'm a brilliant scholar

-Then always remember your **PHD** will stand for,

Paid **H**ighest **D**ollar.

As I wrote this poem, I understand, college is expensive

-Just find a way to keep going, your own personal incentives.

Along the way, you'll earn multiple degrees

-But **PHD**

brings home

The Bacon, & The Cheese!!

Push Through

Have you ever had those moments when you just
don't want to?

The Great ones all have, but they **P**ush **T**hrough.

Have you ever had that quitting feeling compelling
you?

I did while writing this book, but you're reading it
now, because I **P**ushed **T**hrough.

Have you ever felt you couldn't do something
because of what someone told you?

Have you ever **P**ushed **T**hrough to make their
words untrue?

Have you ever had a dream you felt couldn't come true?

Have you ever **P**ushed **T**hru all the obstacles to make that dream come true?

Such an Awesome and Exuberating feeling to know you kept control,

When it took so much demand, just to PUSH THROUGH, to achieve your goal

You're not finished, you're Not THROUGH, complacency wants to conquer you.

Push **T**hrough fears, Push Through doubts,

PUSH!

To Get Your GIFTS OUT!!!

Slow Readers

Slow readers, have no fear, your lyrical genius is

here.

Let's hangout and go places, let's make some

reading fears disappear.

My formula is hip and crazy,

Take some journeys with me and your reading

speed can grow greatly.

Just don't be lazy.

I was a slow reader until age 17,

That's when I got introduced to rapping and my

reading became more keen

I had no clue to what was happening, I had to

read sentences to a beat.

I couldn't pretend and I couldn't cheat.

There was Never Ever a moment that I felt I

couldn't do it.

Being a slow reader wasn't going to make me

unfit or quit.

Preparing for a talent show, the more I rapped

and the more I read,

My reading comprehension increased instead.

Totally oblivious to what was transpiring,

Reading rhymes brought a competence I was

acquiring.

Reading rhymes has never lost its magic,

But taking it away has proven to be tragic.

I guess some smart people decided the age that

rhyming wasn't valuable.

Many rappers would probably say that's quite

fallible.

If great read rhyming books were designed for

teenagers and adults,

I believe America would have better reading

results.

My Fellow Slow Readers, hang with me, journey

with me throughout this book,

And I believe your reading speed &

comprehension, can have a different look.

Great reading experiences are trapped,

because your greater reading comprehension,

is still untapped

Stay Fresh Baked

Invest in Yourself

You are human capital

Empower yourself

You're worth money

Like venture capital

Stay fresh baked

Meaning...

Learn new ways

To do old things

Always be in It

TO WIN IT

The View

The View from here is always nice,

I had examined the rich then I examined my life.

See Middle

Class status

was always

Chill,

But the income

I made

didn't pay rich Bills.

Living like the wealthy a decision of mine,

I stopped procrastinating

started writing down

RHYMES!

Many

occupations

can make a

man

RICH,

It's time you

Move Upward,

Keep Finding

Your Niche.

The View from here is incredibly nice,

Buying what you want, whatever the price.

Luxury,

travel,

stop being

afraid,

It's time you

figure Out,   *HOW TO*

Go Get Paid!

I'm not talking about a 9 to 5,

Living check to check just work to survive.

Use your ideas, Pursue That Life You Crave,

Don't be like the dreamers

Taking dreams to the grave.

126

The View from here
is simply nice,

Successful people
will give you,

this bit of advice.

Don't let your
dreams die,

create a

PLAN OR TWO.

Every time a dream dies, that part of you dies too.

Whether young or old, boy or girl,

Birth your dreams into this world.

& So what you've been down,

GET UP!

SHOW THE WORLD WHAT YOU CAN DO!

Go & become my neighbor,

So we can sit and chat.

About

The View...

Watching

Watching others with less talent than you,

-watching some make their dreams
come true.

Watching friends pursue their college
degree,

- watching foes become the best they
can be.

Watching TV, you see so many things
new,

- watching an idea you had,

that has come true.

Watching your idea start small and then
Burst!!

-And one day you say,

"I had that idea first."

Every idea that will ever come true,

will come from someone

with the idea.

Someone Just Like You!

Don't Spend Your Entire Life,

WATCHING.

Your Story

Your life is your story.

Live it with purpose, honor and glory.

Every life is different,

frame by frame.

Could look similar,

but two aren't the same.

Live the story you want to tell,

Legacy comes from your story as well.

When you're long gone,

    what will people say?

Will kids tell their kids,

    that you passed this way?

It's your journey,

    your very own path,

        Every decision you make,

        has aftermath.

Life will pass by in a hurry,

    And every last creature,

        lives its very own story,

What Will Your Story Say?

1 Two 3 Liners
Motivational LYRICS (to live by)

Greatness doesn't have to be a dream,

Find your magical thing!

Being Great Is a MINDSET, and so is Being Median

If you don't want to be great, No Worries, YOU WON'T BE!

At 65 I still go to the gym almost every day,

intense,

who am I competing against?

For more chances to be outstanding at something,

Process Awesomeness,

in All Things!

GREATNESS is non-transferable,

you have to get it for yourself...

Why think about exercising??

Thinking about it only allows you to think your way

out of it.

Less Thinking... More Starting!!

Healthy living is like brushing your teeth,

Do It Daily!!!

When Desire for Greatness Is your Character,

Accepting Less,

IS OUT OF CHARACTER!

I was **_CREATED_** for GREATNESS!!!

How will you Teach Your Children To Be Great?

If you always ate the Mediocre Bait?

Dreams for middle-class you advocate, but your

Child's Big Dreams, you unconsciously Subjugate.

You bought the Mediocre Mindset,

now you sell and regurgitate,

Dreams of Wealth and Riches,

CAN'T BE THEIR FATE.

Your aspirations and your dreams you have to

protect them.

Family and friends dim your brightest gems.

They want everyone humdrum,

Just Like Them.

Create your own destiny in life,

no matter what your mother or father did,

or didn't do...

Homeless because many tries flopped,

Shouldn't Stop You from reaching the mountain TOP!

FAILING IS PREPARING YOU 4 WINNING!

No one ever told me I can be Great.

But I DISCOVERED

no matter your age, You Can Be…

You can nibble on successful crumbs for life

or learn to fill your plate.

It's an easy choice

to be mediocre,

but another fate

can await.

Go Be Great!!!

She's a Boss!

That little girl in your class has risen to the Top!!

Dream **L**adies **D**ream,

Your carousel of success **S**hould **N**ever **S-**Top!!

136

Your Altitude is a product of your Attitude.

& Your Attitude is a product of your Belief System.

The **Lion** is **KING** because of what it **Believes** about

itself. To some prey the lion is slow or small,

and even against prey stronger & tall,

The **Lion's COURAGE**

To **Believe**,

Conquers It **ALL!**

Women have the smarts to cover where their Man

may lack,

He has the strong Backbone

but his strong WOMAN,

has his back

Everyone needs someone to tell them they CAN!!

Because the world is filled with people who

will tell them, *They Can't.*

GOOD BYE

MOM'MA

Momma,

Why did you leave me so early?

I can barely remember your face.

Momma why did you leave me so early?

To grow up without you in my space?

My friends would argue with their Moms

   and simply break my heart,

They didn't know my day-to-day anguish, of us being apart.

The memories I have, although they are few,

You were the Greatest Mom Ever;

there will never be another you!

Moms are such a jewel, you were my everything,

My Princess, First Lady and My Favorite Queen!

When I called your name and my fear was at its height,

When I yelled MOMMA!

Everything would be alright.

When I had a scratch

or a bigger cut too,

You would kiss it,

bandage it, and make me brand new.

140

Momma's are God's gift to a child,

To birth us, nurture us, but God takes her home after a while.

Momma,

I never got to say,

I'm sorry if at birth,

& During my years,

I gave you any trauma.

I miss you dearly,

I LOVE YOU MOMMA!

GOODBYE, Best Wishes & Thank You!

Goodbye my friend, you still mean so much to me,

But arguing like teenagers, just can't be.

We should be able to agree to disagree,

Us yelling & screaming with one another,
simply isn't the key.

Communication is conversation with give & take,

Not just trying to get your point across

without giving me space.

To share how I feel, and give my debate.

You captured my heart but keep pushing it

away.

142

I'll cherish our memories and our great times,

But this rollercoaster of love,

my heart doesn't like the ride.

Life is too short, we had so many tries,

I wish you the best of luck,

it's our final…

Goodbye.

I HAVE

Have you fallen for someone totally unexpected
out of nowhere? Just to discover you can't have
them.

I have

Have you ever started feeling a certain kind of way
but every time you would say, they just run away?

I have

Have you ever had to pick your jaw and pride up
off the ground because you wanted them in your
world badly, but their past confounds?

I have

Have you ever had to gather yourself day by day
and wrestle away thoughts of them every day?

I have

Ever tried to continue dating

yet you knew you were unfair?

Because your emotions & thoughts

kept your mind elsewhere

I have

144

Have you ever just wanted to say...

I miss your laughter

I miss our witty exchanges

I miss your voice

I miss getting text messages from you

I miss seeing those pretty eyes too

I miss thinking about you regularly (like daily)

I miss the many smiles you give while together,

I wanted to see your smiles forever

I miss seeing your Sexy Body

I miss learning about your journey

I miss working to better understand you

I miss understanding how to better befriend you

Have you ever avoided saying those things because
they thought it meant attachment & strings?

I have

Have you ever had to walk away from chemistry
you've longed for?

For no solid reason but because of their
experiences from before?

YES,

I HAVE

I HAVE walked away from companionship for love in that friendship. And I genuinely wished them the best in happiness.

I HAVE & Will Honor Friendship

Even when losing them

Hurt So Badly

I HAVE reflected on fond memories

While reflecting

So Sadly

Have you ever Wished & Hoped

To have

Them back....

I HAVE

IT'S ALL ABOUT ME

It's all about me, no more fighting and no more pleads,

No more crying over foolish deeds.

It's all about me now, I've been hurt and I've been down,

No more crying, no more frowns.

It's all about me, and I plan to fulfill my every need,

Explore different doors while I'm doing me.

Since it's all about me, I might have One or I might have Three,

Friends to call, when 1 disagrees.

It's all about me, I don't care what people say,

Going to eat all my cake and get served that one way!

GOD you're my Father and you know who I am,

So please forgive me Daddy, but I don't give a damn

I've been hurt so much, with the cards I been dealt,

Gonna share some pain, share some of what I felt.

I'm ready to play the field, my heart under lock & key,

At this time in my life, IT'S ALL ABOUT ME!!

It's Been a Long Time

Hello there, how are you?

It's Been a Long Time,

I hope that you

& Everyone are doing fine.

Just thought I'd said hi,

since you were on my mind,

It's Been a Long Time,

we both be on that grind.

Not many weeks go by,

              where I don't wish you were mine,

I've wanted to say hi so many times,

but I always decline.

Truth be told,

I'd love to hear your voice,

But I'm afraid to hear you have someone,

afraid you made a new choice.

So, let me get to the point, of my note,

Thinking of you with someone else,

puts a lump in my throat.

It's Been a Long Time,

since we last held and kissed,

It's Been a Long Time since that day,

I made you pissed.

                    I'm trying to reach out

because it's been too long.

I still want you in my life,

I'm sorry, and I was wrong.

I took you for granted,

your love,

your commitment,

and your finance,

              Please forgive me of that stance,

please grant me, one more chance.

Mistakes of a lifetime

When we make the mistake of a lifetime, can we ever
get over the regret?
The person that God personalized for us, we didn't
recognize the duet.
That job opportunity we left on the table,
Giving up on a dream, while still young and still able.

The mistake of a lifetime, that alters the course of your
life,
Have a child while unmarried, then get convinced to
make that parent, husband or wife.
While really loving someone else, deep down inside,
We made the grave mistake of not making our true
love, our true prize

Three lives paralleled for disaster,
Because of bad advice and persuasion from a Pastor.
God is still match making, but we're swayed by others,
We get detoured from the one we love, and leave her a
struggling mother.
Forfeit at will, the life we were supposed to live,
For a non-compatible marriage, driven all uphill.

150

You see...

Some mistakes, are mistakes of a lifetime.
Unfortunately, we only get one time, at this lifetime.
Some regrets we'll ponder, from time-to-time.
But the mistakes where we wish we had changed our mind,
Are the **MISTAKES** that haunt us, **for a LIFETIME!**

Will you have me back

Will you have me back? I made a terrible mistake.

Going out with someone, was the greatest mistake I could make.

I took you for granted, and I'm sorry,

I took you through a dark wilderness, an uncomfortable safari.

Will you have me back? I learned from my mistake,

I meant those things I said, true words and nothing fake.

I never should have gone out with the old friend I bumped into,

But going out with someone different, did confirm what I already knew.

You're the one I want, you make me feel alive,

I want to grow old with you, and share memories, to archive.

You're my best friend and confidant, and that is a fact,

I'll massage your feet as a daily treat, if you'll have me back.

<u>INSPIRATIONAL</u>

Invisible

I was never the oldest sibling
But I was once the youngest child
Then I got showered with love and attention
That would make any child smile

Oh! but then came the time
For a new one to shine
He stole my time
That child committed a crime

No longer the baby
My attention faded
My hugs dwindled to maybe
My visibility, raided

Visit Grandmother's house
Waiting for usual kiss
I'd be placed on the couch
And my kiss, goes amiss

Made invisible
By a kid I barely knew
Hoping to become visible
But then there were two

154

Waiting for kisses
I didn't get that luck
But Who really misses?
Those kisses were yuck

Siblings are divisible
Now nobody sees you
You're now invisible
Your limelight is through

One day before old and gray
siblings say, I looked up to you
Coworkers and friends would also say
Glad I met you

For many years,
You felt Invisible
Then God tells you
You were always visible
To the many you knew
Plus, the countless others
Who grew,
From the visibility of you!

Blessed Beyond Measure (BBM)

I've been blessed beyond measure

While living life driven by my own selfish pleasures

I was still **B**lessed **B**eyond **M**easure

Even with my countless UnGodly endeavors

God faithfully **B**lessed **B**eyond **M**easure

With no scorecard, to put me under insurmountable pressure

We've been **B**lessed **B**eyond **M**easure

With a love that will outdistance, out pace and out measure

Incredibly **B**lessed **B**eyond **M**easure

By a love that will outmatch, outshine and outlast, forever

God's Grace & Mercy goes beyond measure

Although we've provided God innumerable, displeasures

I've been **B**lessed **B**eyond **M**easure

While God was secondary, in pursuit of worldly treasures

Still **B**lessed **B**eyond **M**easure

But truth be told, my human faith was often quite fair weather

Why does God continue to **B**lessed **B**eyond **M**easure?

In the midst of   *Blessed*   foolishness,

in the midst of   whatever…

BEYOND MEASURE

David

David, one of my standout people

in the bible,

because he favored me.

A womanizer very tribal,

with a heart of lust and glee.

But it was something about David,

which GOD loved indeed.

Maybe it's because David said in Psalm 51,

"Wash away all my iniquity and cleanse me from my

sin."

I'm sure that GOD heard David, He Blessed

David

again and again.

David also said in his Psalm,

"Surely I've been sinful from birth when mother

conceived me,"

157

God knew David's heart was in his Psalm,

but with so much power in his palm,

David's fight to live right would flee,

during his lifelong, journey.

We've all played that part,

born sinful from the start,

but David gives us hope.

God said

"I have found David the son of Jesse,

a man after my heart"

Maybe we too,

born sinful from the start,

can still be man or woman,

after God's Own Heart?

David, (like you and I)

sinners from the start

still captured God's heart.

Dear God,

I have never taken time to write my heart out to you,
I have watched and questioned some of the things that you do.
Your endless power created the moon, the stars and the seas,
yet you let certain misfortunes happen to little ole me.
You made life where things don't always go as planned,
I've learned to cherish special moments and hold what I can.
Through tears through laughter and intimate praise,
you've been building who we will be, for days and for days.

Dear God, your craftsmanship I marvel at each day,
to see the birds, the squirrels and kittens at play.
Your spirit gives life, direction, helps us up when we fall,
I know there's a purpose at the end of it all.
You sprinkle your power on those you're appointing,
while we walk around with our unknown anointing.
Despite our sinful ways you wait with arms straight,
A gesture of your grace and unyielding faith. Thank you.

PS. Dear God there's one more thing that I'd like to say,
I'm thankful you made me and made me this way

Don't know how, or why You did it

I was introduced to You as a child

Not knowing my experiences and knowledge of You would begin to compile.

You told me I would find peace in my valleys and storms

As a Youngster, I didn't know if You would show up, how You would perform.

When tragedy hit, You said I would survive

When life's pains were at their greatest peaks, Your comfort always arrived.

Don't know how, or why You did it

Time and time again, Your love stayed committed.

When I got reckless, doubtful and foolish

You displayed Your strength the coolest.

When my back was against the wall

You took over my fight, in every brawl.

You moved mountains, You heard my cries and calls

You changed my character, which was best of all.

Don't know how, or why You did it

I turned my back to You, what made You stay so committed?

160

You've been a way maker for hundreds of millions of people

It doesn't matter if we are in the dirt or in a building with a steeple.

We can choke eating peas or get blindsided on the freeway

But we're here today, simply because, Mercy and Grace.

The body is so intricate, every breath of life is miraculous

Your surgical metamorphosis of a human mind and heart, is also, utterly miraculous.

Your transformation power is individualized

One day we wake up with a better morality, than we realized.

Some change in the twinkling of an eye, some change over time

Strongholds Shackles Bondage, Chokeholds of the mind.

You burst yokes for folks, You cause walls to fall

You sent us a miracle worker, and You sent us the Greatest of All.

A caring Son who lived life who shed his blood who left his story

That little ol me, may one day, immerse,

In Your Grandeur of Glory.

God and Money

We've been hoodwinked, very subliminal,

To believe pursuing wealth, is somewhat criminal.

If you desire to get rich, money is your idol,

Our salvation therefore, becomes suicidal.

Satan distorted our thinking, that money is evil,

But God declared your wealth, and money is waiting

for your retrieval.

To make things more clear, let's set the atmosphere

Jeremiah 29:11 (NIV)

For I know the plans I have for you," declares the LORD,
"plans to **prosper** you and not to harm you, plans to give
you hope and a future

Deuteronomy 8:18 (NIV)

But remember the LORD your God, for it is he who gives
you the **ability** to produce **wealth**, and so confirms his
covenant, which he swore to your forefathers, as it is today

Deuteronomy 5:33 (NIV)

Walk in all the way that the LORD your God has
commanded you, so that you may live and **prosper** and
prolong your days in the land that you will possess

Proverbs 13:22

A good person **leaves an inheritance for** their **children's children**, but a sinner's wealth is stored up for the righteous.

Satan uses tactics to declare money is root to evil:

For the love of money, people would rob from their mother,

For the love of money, people would kill their own brother,

For the love of money, people would sell their own teen,

Just to get that mean lean green.

Your wealth is very important to Satan,

With wealth and power, many lives you will straighten.

He hoped we would never discover God's money words,

Money is a weapon against Satan, so he keeps our eyes blurred.

Ecclesiastes 7:12 (KJV)

For wisdom is a defense even as **money is a defense**, but the Excellency of knowledge is that wisdom shields and preserves the life of him who has it.

Ecclesiastes 10:19 (NIV)

A feast is made for laughter, wine makes life merry, and **money is the answer for everything.**

God said **money** is a **defense,**

So, who do we **defense against**? Our **enemy**

These are actual scriptures, please read them for yourself,

God gave you the **ability** for wealth, time to get it off the shelf.

This he swore to your forefather, you have the ability to produce,

God prefers you to **be wealthy**, then **help others**, to bust loose.

God and Money

God Knows

God knows I'm tired of faking

God knows, I'm tired of taking

God knows I'm tired of playin

He knows, exactly what I'm sayin

God knows I'm ready for something real

God knows, I'm learning patience, to be still

God knows my appetite

He knows, every single thing I bite

God knows I'm still discovering who I am

God knows my past will haunt, to confuse, my need and my want

God knows I'm an expert, at messing things up

He knows my entire above, can hinder sincere love

God knows, I've broken hearts and given strife

Why have I played with things, I should've cherished for life

God knows my highs and God knows my lows

There's a person I'm still trying to find, & God Knows.

Ready for home

I have fought a good fight, I have finished my course,
I laid it all out, very little remorse.
Most times I did right, many times I did wrong,
But this person you made, is **ready for home.**

I don't understand all about the afterlife,
But I believe in your son, Jesus Christ.
I believe my Mom and Dad are home with you,
And countless other people, that I knew.
I believe Jesus shed blood to cover our wrongs,
This good-hearted person, with my many wrongs, is **ready for home.**

I maneuvered through life doing the best I knew,
And discovered human invincibility, is so untrue.
The frailty of humans, and these old bones,
Begin to pop and crack, as time moves on.
I moved the needle for my generations to come,
Planted seeds to be harvested, with my ingenious green thumb.
Got them prepared for my day, to ride to glory on a cloud
Separation will be painful but can they only grieve, for a little while.
I'm tired now, my hair is thinning to comb,
Every day that passes my way, I'm **ready for home.**

I'LL BE BY YOUR SIDE

I give the sun, the moon, and your

Laughter;

Happiness,   Memories,

things that   you're

After

I'll be your shelter through the rain and the

storm;

I'll keep you warm, I'll be by your side

You told me you cared for me, dared to share

love with me;

Romance, intimacy, a pure love story.

My love is so deep for you, and I want you to

know,

I love you so, I'll stay by your side.

167

I'll be by your side to support the dreams you
See,

Walk side by side, then pick you up, if the
dream seems
Bleak.

I give the faith, to trust dreams can come
True,

I'll be by your side, to believe in you, and
encourage you
Through.

Remember your shelter through the rain and the
Storm,

Come inside, hold on tight, I'll keep you
Warm.

I'll always be there for you, even when everything seems
Blue,

I won't leave you, nor forsake you.
I'll Be By Your Side.

JUST POETRY

Memories

Memories are those special moments in life

Where a snapshot of time, may or may not,

get captured by a device

But that moment in time, leaves an indelible mark

A data package worth having stored in your heart

Memories are etched on our internal hard drive

To be captured and filed, and available to archive

Memories can carry emotions, most of them do

There are good ones and bad ones and sad ones
too

The fond ones get the most reflection

And seem to get shared with the most affection

Memories made with love in the heart are Prize-

Winning

Memories are made at birth during Life-Giving

Memories made with family at the holidays bring

Thanks-Giving

But Memories made with your lover are

The Most Award-Winning!!

&

The Most Superlative Part About Memories

Are....

Making Them!!

171

MORE THAN SKIN DEEP

The depth of my beauty is deeper than skin deep,

The depth of my beauty is available to reach.

Beyond just your eyes, my world lives inside.

A world filled with bumps & bruises all taken in stride.

The glow on my skin, it starts from within  Just reach a little deeper, & ask to come in

You'll learn of my ups & downs & places I've been.

You'll learn many times I lost. BUT, most times I Win!

Come look a little deeper, past just my skin,

I'll share my cool journey. Simply, ask to come in.

172

Free

Free to be me

Free to do me

Free to feel free

Free to discover me

Free from mate

Free of weight

Free to feel free

Free to date

Free from job

Free from Bob

Free to feel free

Excited to explore me

173

Free from drama

Free from trauma

Free to feel free

Spend all day in pajamas

Free from tears

Free from fears

Free to feel free

& Sexually, learn to express me

Free from my past

Free from my last

& Life's box I was given

Free to live in contrast

I'm Free,

  & It feels Amazing!

  2 Be

   & Feel

    FREE...

IT'S A BABY GIRL! IT'S A BABY GIRL!

I L-O-V-E, Y-O-U, my baby girl;

Thanks for showing me beauty, in a mean old world.

You opened doors I thought were closed;

You put back warmth where my heart was cold.

A relationship that was almost done;

You bring us hope, joy, and lots of fun.

You made avenues out of dead-end roads;

A new beginning ready to unfold.

I L-O-V-E, Y-O-U, my baby girl;

You're more beautiful than a sunrise,

You're more precious than a pearl.

I see so much potential in you, there's nothing you can't do;

I hope you make your biggest dreams, all come true.

I'll always be there for you and try to give you the world;

You know I love you baby, you'll always be,

DADDY'S BABY GIRL!

I LOVE YOU ASHON

NBA

I love the NBA,
I love the game they play,
Today's basketball,
and hoops from back in the day.

I love the 3-point splash, I love the no look pass,
Players that kick much ass and players that talk BIG trash!
Women come to the games in high heels and pearls,
Basketball players get the loveliest girls.

I love the NBA, the artful game they play,
Wizardry with the ball, this art is here to stay.

I love the Alley Oop off the pick roll,
Then the monster dunk, that makes the crowd go
WHOOAA!!!.
They do charity work helping day by day,
Super Fan-Tastic is the N-B-A!!

S-C-E-N-T of a LIONESS

Majestic Beauty

The LION

and the LIONESS!

Stoic, Fearless, Cunning,

Family-Bloodline,

Decisive,

Unhesitating, Forceful, Smart,

Prideful, Powerful,

Assertive, Unyielding, Tough, Dominant,

Confrontational,

Protector,

Fierce,

Resolute

and Live Daily…

Prepared for the

Battlefield of War!

But there is much more about this feline we can adore.

They are the only cat species with the brilliancy to create

and live in a social community.

A community with a KING(s) and a Queen with babies, grandmothers, aunts, cousins and side chicks. Because of their brute strength and merciless savage hunting style, man overlooks their grandeur in their genius. Living in a social family structure of a community with rules and harsh correction is quite complex. I don't know where the LIONS IQ test ranks against other animals but the LION very seldom if ever gets in the conversation of intelligent creatures.

Characteristics of the LION and the LIONESS easily make them many peoples most Beloved animals. And just like people, no two LIONS or LIONESSES have the same DNA, each has their own personality and character. Some are more Romeos and some are more Warriors, some are more Brilliant and some are Mobster Notorious. Nevertheless, God created them quite uniquely with a little something special. The Bible is also crafted with 10 Bible verses that liken God to a LION. Perhaps this is significant and not a bungle, LIONS have garnered the name, "KING of the Jungle". And what makes them KING of the Jungle, when they don't live in the Jungle? They usually reign in open plains. They wouldn't be the largest animal in the jungle, probably wouldn't be the smartest animal in the jungle, they wouldn't be the heaviest animal in a jungle, but wherever they show up, everything else…. RUNS!!! The LION possesses an attitude that makes every other animal, fearful of them.

And then for the LIONESS, we must also add Loyal, Planners, Strategist, Crafty, Clever, Graceful, Skillful, Agile, Hunters, Subservient, Meal Preparer, Mother and Nurturer. Although the LIONESS isn't the KING on the throne, The LIONESS, is in a class all her own. And the KING understands, her role is a great perk, she's the glue that makes his Pride Work. And in her own way, she protects the male KING(s) also. The savvy hunting prowess she brings provides the food needed for the entire pride, including the KING. The LIONESSES are the primary hunters while only weighing about 300 pounds compared to her male counterparts 450 pounds. The LIONESS guides and watches over the pride so they have to grieve a pride member's death, more in stride. She also provides the KING's support system and covering when he's been wounded from battle and she reaffirms the prides stability when he's been rattled. KINGS are prepared to battle regularly with challenging male LIONS

180

trying to invade their territory or duel for their pride. The KINGS primary role in the pride is to mate and continually monitor and scent the perimeter of the pride's territory. They walk their perimeter for days or weeks at a time protecting their home, their family and their property from their enemies and their rivals. When he returns the LIONESS & pride feel comforted. The LIONESS has an uncanny way of knowing when to enter into his space, when to caress, and when to stay in her place. Then sadly, there will always come a time when a KING doesn't return. The LIONESS life & pride's world become much more stressful & difficult then. The LIONESSES will have to move on and safeguard their pride. Knowing when a new KING comes to reign, for all male cubs, death is applied. The death of a LIONESS' cub puts her in heat to mate with the new KING to start his own royal bloodline.

S-C-E-N-T of a LIONESS

seductive

Strong

Courageous

Educator

Nurturing &

Talented

= her Individualized

Unique **SCENT**

181

The LIONESS is truly an amazing animal. Not nearly as strong as the dominant male LION, but a very magnificent creature. She runs circles around her male counterpart when it comes to hunting successes, and she's the hunting teacher. A LIONESS

uses much more tactical expertise and precision. She dominates the male when it comes to hunting decisions and making food provision. As the main meal provider, she can masterfully take down animals 5 times her weight. She manages the youth and will give her body to the KING, every 20 minutes to mate.

The **S-C-E-N-T** of a LIONESS is tantalizing and mesmerizing. She can throw the LIONS focus off because her aroma is irresistibly appetizing. She puts the male LION on an invisible leash, and has momentary power over him until he unleashes. When a young LIONESS is ready to start her own pride, her **S-C-E-N-T** becomes polarizing. She wants lovin and her body begins advertising. Hoping for an up-and-coming KING, with a warrior spirit, to create her offspring. Every LIONESS wants to generate a bloodline from a gladiator. So, his fighting ability and his heart is that indicator. If he runs from the battle with a quick flight, he will not be able to mate her because of his fright to fight. Every LIONESS wants the heart of a champion and for that she has no guilt. She knows many intruders will come and try to take what they've built.

She really checks his heart before she will mate, she has the foresight to wonder about the later date. Will her mate be a good protector, backbone and strength of her family? Will her mate be consistent and courageous through difficult times? Will her mate protect their perimeter when an intruder crosses the line? Will her mate give her support when the two of them have to align?

Many think the reason why LIONS are considered KING, has more to do with the attitude LIONS bring. Soldier/Assassin Mentality & their Gangster/Thug Attributes: a retaliative spirit, competitive nature, gutsy, family-centered, intelligent and always prepared to take life. LIONS are lionhearted and will fight to the death, they will go out swinging until their very last breath. The male LION also boasts a royal mane around his neck, him getting choked out during battle isn't usually a threat.

The **S-C-E-N-T** of a LIONESS

And her many humanistic tendencies,

Always nurturing her offspring, for independency.

She's the Hero that goes unsung,

And she is fiercely, protective of their young.

The LION operates a family structure design, which resembles mankind. The KING of BEAST gets comforted, nourished, reaffirmed and his children taken care of by his women. LION KINGS value their QUEENS and her Royal Highness, they follow The **S-C-E-N-T,** of the Magnificent LIONESS.

She's That Kool Kat!

Time with you

My time with you Was So Marvelous!!!

The time with you Was Remarkable and Riveting!!!

My time with you was Pleasing and Priceless!!!

Time with you is Always Memorializing!!!

My time with you lifts me when I'm feeling blue.

Our bond grows too

Every moment I'm lucky enough to spend time

With You...

185

Spending Time With You,

Is So Satisfying and So Worthwhile,

It's What I Truly, Enjoy To Do!

Simply,

Spending As Much Time As I Can,

With You...

Why Do Good Girls
Like Bad Boyz???

Their innermost being is lured by excitement,

An overwhelming zeal and passion for the daring,

With the mystery of uncertainty, and their security on the edge,

Then, the voluptuous heart conquers wisdom.

<u>*NO!!*</u>

The essence of danger draws their appeal!

Intrigued by excitement,

challenge,

and more daring thrills!

It's the fun that's enjoyed, like brand-new toys…

<u>*&*</u>

That's why GOOD GIRLS, LIKE THOSE

SEX AND ROMANCE

(*R*ated *S*teamy)

A Kiss

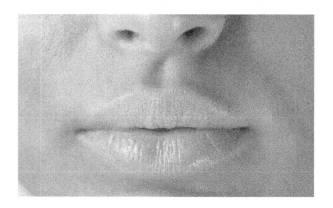

It began with a kiss placed gently on his lips,

And he placed his hands, gently on my hips.

I knew what to do to get him to want me,

And turn our date into a night of ecstasy.

I took his hand and placed it on my breast,

He put it in his mouth and began to caress.

My body reacted to his touch with pleasure,

He explored the depths of my ocean, diving for

my treasure.

While tasting me, I felt his fingers go inside

My love juice erupted and I was ready to ride.

I got on top moving my body under his spell,

His erection grew inside me and the enjoyment

made me **Y**ell!

I screamed aloud when I reached my peak!

He moaned in unison as his body lay weak.

Now here I lay with eruptions thru my body,

REFLECTING

How

he

annihilited **ME**

It all started with a simple kiss,

A

Kiss

That grew into a passionate night,

filled with

FIREWORKS

&

BLISS!!

Umm...

That

KISS

Adam and Eve
(Naked & Not Ashamed)

On the seventh day the heavens and earth were complete,

God rested on that day, after creating His global masterpiece.

After God created man, He placed him in the Garden of Eden, without a madam.

God placed man there for some specific reasons, and called his name Adam.

Everything God created was innocent and pure,

Yet He designed a competitive system, where the best will procure.

Strength and vulnerability, He put both in place,

He gave beauty and quickness and speed and grace.

But **NO** Creation, on land or sea, was created

To Feel Naked and Ashamed.

Everything was procreation, uninhibited, and untamed.

Courting rituals designed differently for all wildlife,

But everything was created with an innate knowledge,

to reproduce life.

Each species with God given insight to mate with its own kind,

The eagle nor hawk nor the wolf nor the fox tried to combine.

Some creatures put on beautiful displays, others seem to caress
one another,

Countless rub bodies together and many smell and lick on each
other.

Free unadulterated intimacy, created by God for God.

Intricate reproduction for every living thing, masterfully unflawed.

Adam would watch animals court and mate to create new birth,

He probably marveled, watching everything replenish the earth.

Adam witnessed love from a mother and her cubs,

He saw unabated mating, in the open and in the shrubs.

God entrusted Adam so much he brought every living
      creature to him,

Then gave Adam the authority to name each of them.

Adam naming God's animals was an Amazing
      and Incredible Feat,

Observing God's circle of life, as it's becoming complete.

But Adam only had God's love to feel,

He started alone in Eden, commissioned to do God's will.

Adam wasn't immediately commissioned to replenish the
      earth.

When timing was right, God knew what Adam's loss of a rib
would be worth.

Man's rib would be the initiation, to multiply man's population,

And God gave human civilization, dominion over all His creation.

Man made a little lower than the angels, at creation's foundation,

God established nature's formation, for earth's duration.

In Genesis 2:18 God said, "It is not good that the man should be alone."

So, God made man a helper while he slept, from man's very own bone.

God felt man was ready for a woman, to learn to love and to mesh.

When Adam awoke, he said, "This is bone of my bone,

and flesh of my flesh."

I imagine Adam and Eve smelled each other's scent and smelled each other's hair,

They were not ashamed to touch, kiss, Nor

lick each other everywhere.

Nature and nurture uninhibited as husband and wife

Walk Around Bare.

Printed in Genesis 2:25: And the man and his wife were both Naked, and Were Not Ashamed.

Some people believe man and woman naked meant

only spirit of man,

Because in God's image, God created man, but was Butt Naked
really God's Plan?

Some believe Genesis 3:21 means God gave man skin after man's
fall caused strife.

But in Genesis 3:21 the CEV version reads,

"Then the LORD God made clothes out of animal skins for
the   man and his wife."

Also, Adam saying "flesh of my flesh" would signify,

They walked around butt naked in flesh, obeying God's charge,
"Be Fruitful And Multiply".

Nudity and Human Flesh were NOT Designed to be immoral
or shameful.

After man ate the forbidden fruit, then they

felt naked and became blameful.

Adam blamed Eve and Eve blamed the serpent

but they both ate.

Shameful nudity entered into man's mind in his fallen state.

197

Before the fall, Naked and Not Ashamed was Understood.

Because everything God created, God said *"**WAS GOOD!**"*

Imagine Man and Woman Unbridled and Untamed,

Loving from head to toe, the total body open game,

Why did God place sensations & stimulations in almost every
spot in the body frame?

Because Everything was Unadulterated, open-air mating,
Blissful. And Not Ashamed.

Ummm!!!

Pure Liberating Freedom

LOVING, ALL OVER!

NATURAL

In Nature!

No holding back, no reservations, just explode into the heavenly.

Each time they obeyed God and strived to replenish the earth

Mating was designed with a spiritual connection to soar the galaxy

Human stimulation during mating,

An Indescribable Feeling

Given At Birth

That allows our spirit to Rome into ecstasy

Can you imagine A&E Making Love in the garden on top of

a bed of flowers?

Or rolling around on the sweet scent of herbs during light

rain shower?

Fresh unpolluted air breezing past their bodies &

between her breast,

Midday on many days, with SUPER heightened senses,

during CLIMATIC CREST!

199

The aroma of human mating

soaring through the air,

With God's creation

Unashamed and Fully Bare.

There's a release of liberation

in Love Makin.

Making Love Is liberating freedom,

The Passion of LOVE,

an Intrinsic Vibe,

GIVEN FROM ABOVE

Celibate (pronounced Cela-bit)

Your smarts and physique, makes me want it.

I'm thankful you're patient because I must admit,

I've taken many cold showers

Because,

My body be lit.

It takes all my strength to get so riled, and then just omit.

I really like your game, but is sex your ultimate score?

I've pursued love so many times,

There has always been pain

in store,

I usually feel some hurt,

whenever I choose that door.

I do love your class

Your ass

&

Your witt

But for me right now

Sex

Just ain't it

So, until we commit

I'm sorry

At this moment in time,

I live

Ca Cela-bit.

Cum Over

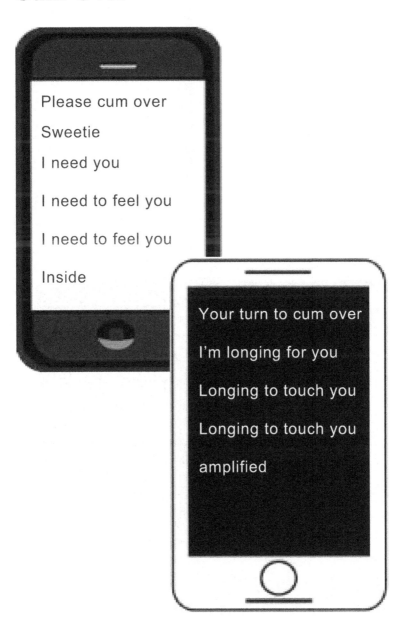

Please cum over

Sweetie

I need you

I need to feel you

I need to feel you

Inside

Your turn to cum over

I'm longing for you

Longing to touch you

Longing to touch you

amplified

A day of tension

And I'm filled up with sum,

We'll both be well pleased,

If you just cum.

Your turn to cum,

Not going to succumb,

My place tonight,

Is where you should cum.

204

Gigolo

I'm the Gig from the past of long ago,

But the people didn't call me a Gigolo.

I was Casanova, Son of a King,

Lady lover to the world, teaching sexy new things.

I gave BIG Explosions, during sexual scenes.

Multiple orgasms, and I mastered that thing.

When ladies wanted real lovin,

I was option number #1.

The Competitive Sport of Love Making,

& Casanova lived Second To None.

Kissing on their feet

& Feel a tingling in their toes,

Let's me know we've arrived,

& she's ready to explode.

Ancestry thru generations

Mastered Sexual Stimulations.

Passed an innate trait to gun for #1.

Start her love juices flowing, with thrilling tongue fun.

205

A long stamina Warrior

An ingenious Gladiator,

I make them all vertex,

The gentle Sexual Educator.

Slow and methodical, patient not swift,

I'm the Heir to Casanova,

& I work the graveyard shift.

The Seed with his spirit from long ago,

Getting paid for my trade.

Now they call me,

Gigolo

I Need You

From the moment I met you I felt such a shift,

You were what I needed to give my heart that lift.

You came in strong opening my eyes to things anew,

Right from the start I realized, I needed you.

Whether you're a friend or a lover it didn't matter to me,

As long as you could play a role in my life to some degree.

I felt I had to guard my heart from unknown hurts that could come my way,

Because Vulnerability comes with a risk, and an expensive price to pay.

Ohhh but your kiss made me weak, it had been years since I've felt desired,

Then with every touch you made, you lit my body on fire.

I tried to fight it but as you went lower licking and caressing my inner thighs,

Not ever has someone made my body convulse and bring tears to my eyes.

Prior to you,

        I lived my sexual life without coming,

You taught me how multiple explosions,

        will be forthcoming.

I like the new me,

        sexy sassy naughty and wet,

A Christian conservative

        that never knew how good sex could get.

You make me feel like a woman again Babe,

        in all that you do,

Without a doubt

        I know deep in my soul,

        I NEED YOU!!!!

Intimacy

*Bold Words Are Male Voice

Hello Handsome, I can't sleep

I need you

next to me

My body keeps

yearning for you

and needs your

INTIMACY.

I want your

INTIMACY

Inside of me,

NOW!

Funny babe,

    I'm lying awake thinking about you,

Your touch, your smell, and guess what?

    I got an erection too.

Umm, that's so flattering,

    you get hard thinking about me?

Did you think about getting me wet

    and letting my juice flow free?

Yes babe,

    that's the method to my passion,

Systematic and discipline

    is my Love Making Fashion.

Meticulous, I like getting you So Wet

    you fart from your juice,

Play inside, play outside

    until significant juice bust loose.

Once I hear the lush slush sound,

    I like swimming with my face,

Moisture on my tongue, my lips,

    as we journey to another place.

210

All juices flowing
        and we don't care where it goes,
Swimming with my eyes closed,
        and feeling your juice on my nose.

Boy, you're the only person

        ever to make all three of my three holes cum,

Your loving is So Crazy Amazing,

        you make my body explode; my juices just succumb.

If a woman never got embarrassed

        because a slushy sound came from her juice,

She's never experienced cumming to the MAX,

        and she never met the person in you.

It's the most exhilarating feeling EVER!!

        How did you Master your Love Making Endeavor?

        Everything you do,

                is so darn clever!

211

INTAMACY

I love
Your conversation,
Your laughter,
and our honesty
is carefree.
But
my favorite
part
of our
INTIMACY,
is feeling
YOU,
inside of
ME.

Seduction

Hello Mister,

long time no talk to,

I hope you be missing me,

the way I be missing you?

Hello Beautiful, I hope all is well,

I do think about you, but I don't let the thoughts dwell.

I want you to cum make love to me your amazingly good way,

I got wet just thinking about seeing you today.

213

I can't do that anymore, sadly,

I'm still attracted to you and I still want you badly.

Then cum and see me just this last time,

I'm so hot for you and you can get home at a good time.

Whenever I cum see you, you have tricks up your sleeve,

And the way you give it to me, I never want to leave.

I just like to make you feel special baby,

I try to be your best lover ever, with no doubt and no

maybe.

That's my problem babe, you're the best lover I've had

in life,

But darn you have a Husband who's a Pastor, and

damn, I

have a  Wife.

I wish we both weren't married, I guess I've become numb,

My husband barely touches me, and he never makes me

cum.

WOW! Making love with you takes my breath away!

He doesn't know what he's missing, my wife doesn't get

down your way.

The many things you do, keeps my head twisted too,

I thought I was the queen of new, but you taught me a thing

or two. Or three.

I guess like so many good things, this must come to an end,

Today will be my last time, we need to break our addiction my friend.

Just cum over baby, let me massage you where you are sore,

I know just what you need, I'll provide what you need and more.

Umm... Umm...

A Few months later.

Hey Mister, long time no talk to. I hope you're missing me...

* Bold words male voice

Sex

Sex is a noun, that's hard to live without,

Some men and women like it so much,

it's all they think about.

Sex is essential in relationship and marriage,

Don't underestimate it, or your marriage will

miscarriage.

Sexual desire and sexual appetite,

Is different for each person and does cause fights.

Be willing to learn how to pleasure your mate,

Keep fiery romance going with fun spicy dates.

Throughout the day, let your woman know you

want her,

Text something sexy and sultry to

her, or call if you prefer.

With that time on the phone, laugh joke

and be corny,

Flirt and tease, but beware, both can get

seduced and horny.

Have you ever been chatting and discovered,

"oh wow, I'm wet"?

The sound of a lover's voice that has power

like that.

Now ladies don't you fret, men play cool

and don't show sweat,

But they're on the phone aroused, and while

aroused, they can also get wet.

Having sex, making love, desires designed

from above,

In that magical moment of intimacy, your body

soars above the doves.

No thoughts of worry,

Relaxed,

Floating thru outer space,

Traveling to embrace a spiritual connection

ready to take place.

Then you lose control and just let

go, of all your faculties,

A freedom occurs, an arousal SO

GREAT, You burst! Into the

heavenly.

Humans, call it SEX. God calls it, Mate-ing...

Stable

Madam,

To stay rock stable

Keep 3 or 4 enabled

So, you'll always have 1 or 2 ready

For galloping smooth & steady

Keep your thoroughbreds lathered ready to

perform

So, when it's ShowTime, they're always in rare

form

Ready for action, Preakness stakes

Each racehorse wants to win the KY Derby. Make

no mistake

Keep stallions in your stable

Ready and able

Kick start their motors

Like jumper cables

Put the right pedigree in the stable

Some breeds are aggressive and more

unstable

You want Bold & Beautiful that possess

Great Muscle

When the spotlights on, all business all

hustle

Galloping,

You need 1 or 2 always able

So, keep 3 or 4 in the stable

So your stable stays stabilized.

& Your needs,

never go deprived

What you doin to me?

What you doin' to me

I implode into ecstasy

Who are you?

I've never met anyone like you

How do you do this to my body

You're a perfectly blended toddy

Perfect caress in your love making process

You express methodically your moves with finesse.

I've been the schmuck in control

Control the explode

Now excitement climbs

With a new paradigm!

New mountain peaks

Wetland Cheeks!

Then I melt...

Like chocolate in the sun

Loving dealt

Leaves me speechless and stunned

& Not ANYONE!!

Else, I want to see.

You captivated ME!!

HIP HOP MEMOIRS

Hip Hop Memoirs
(Real stories by real people)

Allow me to introduce myself

Real stories taken off the memory shelf.

Hip Hop Memoirs a platform where non-fiction

Stories are shared in a rhythmic rhyme depiction.

Sensational events written in poetry form,

A literary concept, poised to take the world by
storm.

Interviewees share traumatic incidents

that scarred them for life

A catastrophic episode that shaped a life

A horrendous saga of ongoing abuse in life

A devastating injustice that changed one's life

A wartime warrior, with a marred life

And the concrete jungle… always taking life.

226

Webster Memoirs: a historical account or biography written from personal knowledge.

Wikipedia Memoirs: a collection of memories that someone writes about moments or events.

Hip Hop Memoirs:

Captures the heart and essence of the stories shared.

Reproduce the stories to deliver them

In a wordplay story-telling flare.

Hip Hop Memoirs

May be weary for the faint of heart,

But designed to hear the heart, and chronicle its history in a form of art

Hip Hop Memoirs,

Designed with every reader in mind,

Slow readers fast readers and those who appreciate some graphic design.

Hip Hop Memoirs

Where we interview people

Listening for gemstones

&

Stunning pearls.

Real Stories,

Using the Mother Goose Rhyming Concept

But…

it's for

The adult boys and girls.

Going out blazing

When that day

and that moment comes,

The heart beats intensively!

Like pounding on a drum.

It's when blazing, meets wit.

And you really can't prepare for it.

To experience a moment so amazing,

Between life or death,

and you choose...

To **Go Out Blazing**.

Quietly with guns drawn,

    cops have your house surrounded,

Killing you would be justified,

    and totally founded.

You can betray your friends,

    and never make amends,

Or **Go Out B**lazing,

    to where it all ends.

"Come out with your hands up," cops were yelling,

I was young and dumb,

    and blazing was more compelling.

When that day and that moment arrive,

    It's like slow motion.

        All bull shit aside!

You see about 9-gun barrels pointed your way,

    What do you do?

    What do you say?

Defiant and courageous, I came out my way,

Cursing and screaming,

    not once considering,

        I could die that day.

I was a teenage kid that didn't know what to do,

But once your adrenaline hits its peak,

    your instincts consume you.

Somehow,

    I'm still living,

        and for that, God gets the Glory.

I don't know why I'm alive, to share these stories.

One of my friends,

    a big muscle guy named Dave,

Went out blazing,

    and now resides in his grave.

231

Dave got my same adrenaline rush one day,

and he didn't sway.

He too said "fuck it!"

Going **O**ut **B**lazing today.

With his pistol in his hand, police had him trapped,

I don't know if he was

scared

or if he just

snapped.

For a split second

you process that life is

unfair and unjust,

So, it's no trepidation, when living is a bust.

Once life takes you to the edge,

and all hope is tapped,

There is no more fear, so, **C**ap **C**ap **C**ap!

232

That life-or-death choice is short in duration,

I'll always remember that out-of-body stimulation,

    and the mind-altering sensation.

Most will never understand,

    nor will ever feel,

When the mind doesn't process,

    the bullet to blood ordeal.

For a moment, you're an invincible super hero,

    a cartoon sur-real.

Programmed by a cultured world

    that you can't be a punk,

So,

    whenever your heart is challenged,

    your response is to debunk.

It doesn't matter if it's boys in the hood,

or police in uniform,

In the concrete jungle,

a vicious jungle,

fierceness,

is the norm.

Dwelling in a world

Always

Prepared for violence or death,

Produces youngsters

READY

To **G**o **O**ut **B**lazing,

For their very last Breath...

Youngster (marital mischief)

At age 19 he got introduced to a marital affair,

He never imagined such a thing; never thought he
would dare.

With a stylish appeal and a different kind of flair,

But totally green to that thing, yet the married woman
didn't care.

She laid out the rules, and taught how the game

would be played,

"If you see me with my husband, just play cool,

don't be dismayed."

He couldn't get too lovey-dovey nor be smothering to
her,

She would control rendezvous and how often they'd
occur.

She had NO IDEA; she was speaking his language.

He was prepared to give no drama, no anguish.

Allowing her to be Boss, he's willing with no blocking.

Understanding his single life stays in tack,

while their hot passionate lovin is rocking.

All her boxes got checked, yes yes yes,

But she wasn't quite prepared,

for the youngster's finesse.

Endearing and captivating was his forte,

Entrancing was always his mission,

during preliminary foreplay.

Chess had prepared the young athlete to be a

student of every game.

Chess, a game where every move, requires strategic

aim.

A competitive self-driven prodigy,

Who knew nothing about astrology.

236

But built with a nature to perfect his craft,

He studied her every movement and developed her,

the perfect spacecraft.

A ballistic capsule designed to outdistance,

So, when she slept with her husband, her young lover hoped,
she gave him passive resistance.

Her young lover possessed an athlete's mentality,

to be the very best,

If he could take her to the unknown, he'd surpass her
husband's lovin, and the rest.

After studying and availing her, one day,

something intriguing did arise.

While on a double date, she couldn't handle the rules,
which she had applied.

She took him to an enormous nightclub, filled with
beautiful women, That Were Killin!

He followed her rules to a tee, and he was like a kid on
a ride, That Was Thrillin!

Reiterating her autonomy & space before heading to the club,

She didn't want him suffocating her there, like a rookie, or a scrub.

Surprisingly, she watched her young lover maneuver, like a dominant lion cub.

She watched him dance and laugh and she felt slightly snubbed

The youngster was totally oblivious his mistress was watching his success.

She was becoming unraveled, a little pissed and angrily stressed.

It was a long ride back that night.

This youngster she chose, has her feeling quite contrite.

Her friend said "you're lucky you had her keys; she would have left you there. "

The youngster didn't have a clue, on why she was feeling blue with despair.

He gave her the space that she required,

And thought she had the wonderful time she desired.

But seeing her young lover's bravado on full display,

Made her feel insecure, and certain, he would stray.

She realized, her rules and control, bit her on the butt
on that day.

She thought good lovin, would leave him young and
sprung, and she'd lead the way.

Instead, she saw a kid in a candy store,

a youngster, skillfully debonair,

And she knew he and his buddy, would voyage back
there.

A Youngster, Getting Into Marital Mischief.

Time after time married women he met.

He didn't know why, but he kept noticing an asset.

You can have crazy mad sex with them,

Then show up at the club with another fine gem.

They made the rules, and it was rules he invited.

No lovey-dovey, no getting overly excited.

If we see each other out, it's no hard feelings.

The mistresses made these relationship dealings quite
appealing.

The youngster treated each lady with care and detail
and his respect never varied.

Now, a 20-year-old military soldier didn't know the
allure that he carried.

Totally taken by surprise when a beautiful 26-year-old
wife said, "let's get married"

He stumbled on words a bit, "you're not free", he also
thought. How complimentary.

He replied, "how could that be? How could you really
get married to me?"

240

A Youngster, Getting Into Marital Mischief.

Then came a time in Germany, Sexy Brown was
adamant with her rules.

She warned the youngster, and explained, "These are
the rules, for the jewels."

Again, he agreed, and thought WOW! Life is great!

I get to eat the ice cream and enjoy the cake.

His friend had earlier challenged him and said,

"SB was off limits,"

A gorgeous Army Sergeant all business no gimmicks.

"You cannot connect with her, she's a boss, already on
lock down,"

The youngster worked his magic with all the knowledge
he had now compound,

And to his own surprise, he did capture Sexy Brown.

In his competitive seductive way,

he was planning to take her on flight.

Sexy Brown had said with intention,

"This is only for one night."

Viewing him as just a youngster, with energy for a fun night,
but expecting nothing out-of-sight!

But he knew differently, and prepared for her to feel

every ounce of his might.

While priming her mothership to take flight,

the destination,

a newfound cosmic height.

A one-night stand that took her breath away,

Then something happened as they lay.

She wanted more, so maybe her rules could sway,

But she didn't tell the youngster,

that what he sent her way,

Was challenging her thinking,

But she never did say.

242

Day by day, she heard no word from the youngster.

She pondered, had she made a blunder?

Had she met boy wonder?

Could such rules lead to a heartbroken fool?

He didn't know she had these thoughts

but he knew, she had her rules.

Although her rules were stiff,

they were like a gift,

the perfect tool.

Marital mischief became an instrument that the
youngster never imagined,

Giving of himself and still having all his freedom,

would become in fashion.

So, the irony was, the ladies laying out the rules,

Became the culprits,

lacking readiness,

to adhere to the rules.

243

Weeks go by and Sergeant Sexy Brown sees him out

clean and shaved.

He's at a night club and he salutes her with

hello and a wave.

Sexy Brown couldn't handle watching him showcase his

swag in front of her.

Hidden emotions and feelings inside,

began to bubble and stir.

Sergeant Brown got more irate minute by minute as

her fire lit.

Something was there inside

but

she's unwilling to admit it.

She feels like this scoundrel isn't playing fair.

She didn't anticipate watching his magnetism,

would be more

than she could bear.

She felt offended and stunned

because she didn't garner his attention.

But in her rules,

not eliciting his attention in public,

is what she mentioned.

The youngster following her playbook,

which usually proved smartest.

Left her perplexed,

is he a 21-year-old novice?

Or a 30-year-old con artist?

Leaving noticeably upset and steaming,

The first moment she got,

she called the youngster,

cursing and screaming!

Totally baffled and completely surprised,

That she was calling him every name imaginable,

while she chastised.

Mystified,

because she's beautiful and accomplished.

He asked, "What's this from?"

As she kept calling him everything under the sun.

The words didn't bother him at first

but she finally found the magical one.

She finally touched a nerve,

when she used the word,

"Hoodlum."

Changing his direction

his old thug life was dead,

Hoodlum pierced him more

than anything else she said.

"That's not fair" he exclaimed!

"I'm not a thug anymore."

Those words hit a cord,

because of his many mistakes

behind that door.

"Why are you saying these things to me,

what did I do to you?"

She replied

"I saw you and wanted you

and thought you wanted me too."

"You ignored me

as if I was a nobody to you,

But we've been with each other

so I know that can't be true."

"I'm sorry about my rules I imposed,

I should have trusted that you were more mature and

more composed."

After the entire emotional outburst,

she finally faded into his arms,

Finally feeling his warm embrace,

his cool demeanor on display,

was quite the charm.

247

Maybe she learned age and maturity

don't always go hand in hand,

And maybe she learned,

plans to control the heart,

don't always go as planned.

A Youngster, Learning and Teaching,

During Marital Mischief.

But a youngster ensnared. Without a real clue,

on how he really got there.

Voluptuous women

voluptuous rules

untamed freedom,

made his vision impaired.

He went against what he had been taught,

don't do marital affairs.

So many great memories of magical moments

and magical nights with beautiful women,

he never shared.

He never looked to break up a happy home,

he never looked to have someone else's girl,

Perhaps those homes weren't happy homes,

and perhaps their girls, wanted another world.

If he could redo life all over again today,

it would probably go the same way.

The memories they held are unparalleled,

and taught the youngster, his swag compelled,

A youngster who once enlisted, who's way got twisted,

But he never once set out to find,

MARITAL, MISCHIEF.

249

Just Like MY DAD

He didn't come to one game, he always told me he

would come.

Whether baseball, soccer or basketball,

I'd be at my game chewing my gum.

Looking for my pop, putting my head in a tizzy.

"Dad what happened?" "Son I got busy."

Growing up on your own, is what I knew,

Mom dead, Daddy absent, it's the streets and you.

250

Armed robbery arrest, grand theft auto,

Staying out of prison, was hitting the lotto.

Streets take you in, become your best friend,

A drug business at age 13, how does this all end?

My Dad was very special in my heart,

But we'd go months without talking,

without a single remark.

Then all of a sudden, I'm a Daddy too

Guess what I did ……? I did just what I knew.

I had a beautiful daughter and didn't know what to do,

The military option is the option that grew.

Absent from my daughter for her first three years,

I didn't learn her cries, didn't wipe her tears.

My daughter was three and I just began to learn her.

I didn't know her dislikes, nor things she prefer.

Trying to be a good father, but I had little training

So as much as I tried to be different,

the similarities kept gaining,

I missed so many important moments,

then she's a college grad,

Where did the time go?

I did **JUST LIKE MY DAD.**

To my first-born daughter,

please forgive me of my pains,

It wasn't your Daddy's heart,

It was the curse I let reign.

NO Blame Game on the life that I had,

Just one day I realized,

DAMN!

I'm **JUST LIKE MY DAD.**

Some duplications of my Dad,

I don't know how they came,

But whatever pain I caused you,

It's only me to blame.

To each of my children,

Please come share with me

If you will,

About the way I fathered,

and any pain I instilled.

253

I got better at being a Father, to at least be there

Thought my Kids understood, if Daddy's there he cares.

But a Son once told me, you showed up in body,

But emotionally you usually came quite bare.

To all my brothers out there,

whether you're black or white,

Work towards a relationship,

it's well worth the fight.

It's never too late to go back and apologize,

Because life is short,

and everyone dies.

You see my Dad is gone, with all of his fame.

I wish I could ask, "Why'd you miss all my games?"

I would love to hear his voice,

let him clear the air,

And hope he would shoot it to me straight,

on why he wasn't there.

Dad was a Great Giver of Time to the Church,

But for that Troubled Teenage Kid,

That perhaps needed his Dad Most,

Dad was mostly GHOST.

Listen!!!

You can be the Dad,

to break the darn curse,

Of the absenteeism,

that's been well rehearsed.

To all Men and Women with a fractured life as

a kid,

WE STILL GET TO CHOOSE OUR OWN

DESTINY...

NO MATTER WHAT

OUR FATHER DID!!

Thank you for reading & listening.

THE END

OUR BELOVED
BOBBIE L. DANIELS
1937 — 1970
MY FATHERS HOUSE ARE MANY MANSIONS

MOMMA

You Remain My Inspiration

Connect with ME Scan Barcode

Made in the USA
Las Vegas, NV
22 November 2021

35043623R00154